Write to
IGNITE

DEBORAH JOYNER JOHNSON

MorningStar Publications
A DIVISION OF MORNINGSTAR FELLOWSHIP CHURCH
375 Star Light Drive, Fort Mill, SC 29715
www.MorningStarMinistries.org

Write to Ignite
by Deborah Joyner Johnson
Copyright © 2008

Distributed by MorningStar Publications, Inc.,
a division of MorningStar Fellowship Church
375 Star Light Drive, Fort Mill, SC 29715
www.MorningStarMinistries.org
1-800-542-0278

International Standard Book Number: 978-1-60708-252-1

Cover Design: Kevin Lepp
Book Layout: Dana Zondory

FOREWORD BY RICK JOYNER

Debbie is my sister, and I've had a great respect for her writing and editing skills for many years, but I was honestly stunned by the quality of this work. This book is remarkably well done, interesting, and a practical guide for developing and improving writing skills. It will help anyone who reads it. I regret it was not available when I started writing thirty years ago—I have no doubt it would have made a significant difference in my works.

A hundred years ago reading was one of the main sources of education, information transfer, and entertainment. Today television, videos, and movies may have eclipsed books as the primary media. Modern media, like television and journalism, can have a large, immediate impact, but writers continue to have the greatest impact on the world. There is a different power in the written word than in the spoken word. The spoken word can have an immediate impact, but with the exception of rare and uncommon speech, the impact will soon fade. Contrary to this, the written word has longevity and can continue to have impact for generations to come.

For this reason, even the best-known television journalists are rarely remembered long after their careers, unless they are someone like Walter Cronkite. Even this groundbreaking television journalist will likely only be a footnote in history. However, writers are still well-known, as are their works, thousands of years later. Likewise, their works still shape minds and hearts and can leave their mark on every generation after them.

For this reason, the written word deserves to be very carefully crafted. Writers used to be called "wordsmiths" because writing was such an art. With the great competition for attention by all of the other forms of media, writing must be considerably better today if it is going to be read. Like other disciplines and art forms, creative writing has evolved. Overall, it is much better than it was just decades ago. However, there is still a quality found in true classics which lasts beyond their own generation. Classics are not just about the skill of the writing, but also require depth of insight and brilliant articulation. Classics have a message that is timeless.

A timeless message is indeed more than a well-crafted phrase—great ideas and revelations deserve to be well-crafted. For other necessary help developing this most powerful skill, Debbie's book, *Write to Ignite,* is one of the best resources I think you will find to help you to achieve this.

~Rick Joyner

— Table of Contents —

CHAPTER ONE

CREATIVITY IN WRITING

Man's mind stretched to a new idea never goes back to its original dimensions.

~Oliver Wendell Holmes
American author

Why do some books leave a lasting mark, yet others, though well-written, have little or no effect on readers? One major distinguishing factor is the passion of the writer. Passion, which is the result of a deep conviction, combined with the ability to articulate it, is basic to exceptional writing. Passion ignites creativity, but without the essential skills of writing, the writer may not impart the intended effect to the reader.

Writers were once called "wordsmiths" because it was a highly skilled craft. To write something exceptional is not easy—nor should it be. When a writer takes an easy path in writing, the end results will be mundane and disappointing. Those who write with the creativity that passion can spark, with a devotion to excellence in their craft to produce clear, efficient, and meaningful sentences, will wield one of the world's most powerful tools—ideas stated through the written word.

This book was written from the viewpoint of a published writer and professional editor as a guide to aspiring and seasoned writers, not only as a learning tool in the essential skills of writing, but to unleash the creative gift of writing within you.

CREATIVE EXPRESSION

The word *creative* is derived from the Latin word *creatus*, which means to "bring into being." When God created the earth, He brought it into being. We are each given gifts "to bring into being." Many times they are hidden within, and we will have to search to find them. The key is to find those gifts and increase them by using them. Creativity expands through the practiced expression in such crafts as sculpture, painting, songwriting, dancing, and writing. Since everyone is unique, creative expression in the arts will be unique.

Creative expression is as vast as there are people. So how does one develop creativity? Let us begin this study with children. Creativity comes naturally to children. When children play, they use their imaginations to arrive at possibilities which may seem impossible to adults. Albert Einstein was a great believer in the importance of imagination. He said: "Imagination is more important than knowledge. Knowledge is limited. Imagination encircles the world." If creativity at a young age is nurtured, children will begin to stretch their imaginations into problem-solving skills, enabling them to think outside of the box, resulting in creative solutions. Those creative solutions will extend into whatever they do artistically—writing, singing, dancing, painting, and so on.

If children are given ample opportunities to express and develop creativity in writing while their language is developing, their creativity will continue to increase as their language increases. Read the biographies of many great writers, and you will discover that their imaginations were ignited at a young age, causing their creativity to develop early. For example, C.S. Lewis began writing stories at age five. Beatrix Potter began sketching her pets when she was young, and later she wrote stories to complement those illustrations. Yet even if creativity was not cultivated as a child, it is never too late for an aspiring writer to learn to creatively write.

It does seem that some people are born with more creativity than others, but those who begin with less creativity can actually develop as much or more than those with creative gifting simply by being faithful to use what they have. Creativity will develop with perseverance. When I first began writing, I developed headaches from striving to write creatively. I was my own worst enemy at times because I did not feel that I had the creativity to write. However, because of the perseverance to develop my writing, it finally did come. It felt like a bottled spring of water that had at last been released. The more I would write, the more my writing began to creatively flow. I actually became excited and could not wait to see what was going to happen next in my writing. Creativity develops through the active practice of the imagination, which becomes more powerful with use.

A CREATIVE GENIUS

It had long since come to my attention that people of accomplishment rarely sat back and let things happen to them. They went out and happened to things.

~Leonardo da Vinci

To further our study in creativity, we will take a brief glimpse at Leonardo da Vinci, one of the most creative geniuses of all time. By applying what is learned from his life, it will help us to understand how to implement creativity not only in writing, but in all other arts.

As a visionary, da Vinci sought answers to his many questions. Because of his extreme curiosity, throughout his life he studied how objects worked, seeking improvements and new ideas. He did not think about what *is* but what *could be*—he saw possibilities, not hindrances.

9

Though many of his revolutionary inventions and discoveries were far ahead of his time, he demonstrated just how creative a mind could be. Da Vinci was an artist, engineer, scientist, writer, geologist, inventor, and military engineer. The following are just a few of his accomplishments: the first parachute sketched, conceptualized the first helicopter and other flying machines, designed a military tank, sketched the ideal city (with communication, sanitation, and other services), concentrated solar power, an extendable ladder, and the first canal locks ever used.

Da Vinci kept his innovative ideas and sketches in notebooks which he had with him at all times. Pictures in his mind formed from the depths of his imagination, expanding his vision as it was conveyed on paper. He used those blank pages to create pictures to solve problems that plagued his curiosity. As he sketched, new and creative solutions were awakened and generated. He was a master at depositing his innovative thoughts into words and paint. We can learn about the importance of keeping a writing journal through da Vinci's example. All writing begins on a blank page. As the imagination is ignited, new and creative ideas will emerge—not what is, but what could be. When questions arise and solutions to problems are sought, creativity has begun.

CREATIVITY AND TIME

To better understand more about creativity, we will look at two of da Vinci's most famous paintings: *Mona Lisa* and *The Last Supper*. Da Vinci was not afraid to do everything required to make his works masterpieces. Through innovative techniques, with distinctive sensitivity, he made his work come alive in ways not seen before in the age-old art of painting. He was also a pioneer in giving landscape an important role in painting.

In *Mona Lisa* (1503), da Vinci captured light in his brushstrokes to illuminate her expressive face, using darkness in her dress for contrast. Before *Mona Lisa*, portraits were painted full-length. Da Vinci revolutionized painting by introducing the more intimate, hands-folded, waist-up approach, which was imitated immediately. Also previously, the foreground and background were equally distinct. In *Mona Lisa*, she is the focus of the painting, and the background is less distinct. Time and reflection must have guided his hands because it is conjectured by some that it may have taken him as long as ten years to perfect her lips. Many say by studying her face at different angles, a new perspective of her is seen. Some believe Leonardo's mastery in this technique has never been equaled.

Da Vinci's, *The Last Supper* (circa 1498), was resourcefully painted on the back wall of the dining hall at the Dominican convent of *Santa Maria delle Grazie* in Italy to give the illusion of extension to the dining space. Most paintings of the last supper up until da Vinci's painting had shown Jesus blessing the bread and wine with Judas in a corner, many times sulking, with Jesus' other disciples surrounding Him. Da Vinci's painting illustrates a different story. Jesus looks serene as He sits at the middle of the table, but His six disciples on both sides of Him, having just been told that one of them will betray Him, show shock and disbelief. This exemplifies the thought, time, and intricate details that da Vinci created through his perception in this painting.

One of the reasons *The Last Supper* is unique is because it is *not* a fresco. In fresco painting, the artist paints directly onto wet plaster. When the paint intermingles with the plaster, it becomes permanent. Da Vinci experimented with tempera (pigment, egg yolk, and vinegar) and oil paint on dry plaster so he could use more colors and redo parts of the painting if necessary. This new method, however, proved to be an unsuccessful medium for painting on walls. Even while he was still working on it, the painting began to degrade and within a few years, humidity caused some of the paint to peel off the wall. Even so, it proves how da Vinci was willing to take risks and was always looking for new and innovative ways to improve old processes.

Leonardo da Vinci's creative methods were astonishing. To spend years solving the problem of Mona Lisa's lips seems extreme, but it was the amount of time he felt he needed to achieve the perfection he sought in her lips. He once said, "Time stays long enough for anyone who will use it." The value of time is in using it wisely, and he did. The masterpieces, *Mona Lisa* and *The Last Supper,* are still enjoyed today even after hundreds of years. Creativity can come slow or fast—the time it takes is all part of the process. Likewise, in writing, it can sometimes take years to achieve the highest level of creativity, but when it is finally finished, a masterpiece can be the result.

PERCEPTION

Da Vinci once said, "All our knowledge has its origins in our perceptions." Da Vinci's perception of the world around him was objective, so his knowledge was diverse. Perception is our unique view of reality. What we perceive as knowledge can change with new knowledge. One hundred years from now people may perceive what is known in science at this time as foolish, compared to what they will know then. As knowledge changes, so do our perceptions.

If writers write what they know, then what is written will give their unique perception. If an environmentalist writes an article about the importance of recycling with personal examples backing his perception, depth and passion will flow in his writing. If a person who has little knowledge of the importance of recycling writes an article with information not unique to his perception, the article will have no depth or power. Depth comes from writing with passion what we know through our unique perceptions.

Writing must be confident to be believable, which is why it is also important to write what you know. John Jakes, a historical novelist said: "Be yourself. Above all, let who you are, what you are, what you believe, shine through every sentence you write, every piece you finish." When writers are confident in their knowledge, the reader will receive confidence to follow the article or story, which in the end may change the perception of the reader. It is because of this that the media is now considered a fourth branch of government.

Furthermore, creativity is birthed through unique perceptions. When we are convinced about something and passion is ignited from that perception, excitement for that knowledge will be a thread throughout the writing. Curiosity expands the imagination and creativity grows with use. In writing, creativity will spread into new places when the unique perception of the writer finds expression through words.

CREATIVE THINKING, CREATIVE WRITING

You see things; and you say, "Why?" But I dream things that never were; and I say, "Why not?"
~George Bernard Shaw
Playwright, Nobel Prize Winner

Creative thinking enables a person to look at something ordinary and make it extraordinary, stretching the mind into places beyond a typical approach—an idea that was invisible becomes visible. A writer can solve problems with distinctive solutions based on a unique perspective, creating a work of art in the process. Creative thinking is insightful, original, and at times spontaneous, but it cannot be forced. It may take some time for creative thinking to flow, but when it does and it is transferred to writing, an original, artistic work will be produced—the goal of every writer. Practicing creativity in writing is the key to growing in it. The exceptional book is exemplified by skilled writing, flavored artfully with creative expression, and guided by passion.

WRITING AS A CANVAS

When I was writing my fictional book, *The Chosen Path,* scenes with the characters formed in my mind, and I would write words to capture what I was seeing. From my experience in fiction writing, I discovered that writers are artists who paint with the words they use. Just as there are endless, creative ways to paint, there are endless, creative ways to write.

Before the writing begins, the canvas is blank, but soon words will be brushed into a kaleidoscope of colors, igniting the imagination of the writer as the writing builds. The writer will then paint pictures with words. The more skilled the writer, the more clear and vivid the pictures will become. Seasoned writers keep their readers in mind by trying to paint pictures they can see clearly. Subsequently, readers will paint pictures in their imaginations from what the writer has written. Artfully written, words will open the eyes into diverse places that exist only within the perception of the writer and those who can follow where the words lead. If the reader can embrace and be guided by the words, it will seem as if they are experiencing the picture being painted right before them. The words become lifelike, which in turn causes the book to come to life.

Words are used as the catalyst to bring readers to the place created by the writer. Some books are so strategically and creatively written, and readers become so involved in the book, they do not realize they are reading words. The author has convinced the reader that what is written is true through the perception of his or her knowledge. When this occurs, that book will affect readers deeply and it will likely be read and reflected upon as if they had participated in real events.

Where the spirit does not work with the hand, there is no art.
~Leonardo da Vinci

CHAPTER TWO

WRITING THEN AND NOW

The farther backward you can look, the farther forward you can see.

~ Winston Churchill,
Prime Minister of the United Kingdom (1951–1955)

To understand where we must go, we must understand where we have been. Looking back teaches us about the past, the lessons learned there, and how to move forward from that place. Writers who have preceded us have opened our eyes to new ideas and changes in writing. Writers today have the same opportunity to write new ideas with originality and creativity, leaving a path for other writers to follow.

Although there are many insightful books from the past, the style of writing has changed. Granted, authors from years ago were paid by the page, which contributed some to the length of books, but the style of writing was also to write with elaborate details. A prologue (introduction) was once commonly written in fiction and even non-fiction, giving the reader detailed background information before the main scene, event, or information would be given. Life was slower paced years ago, and people enjoyed reading intricate details.

In the era before television, people were drawn to detailed writing because the visualization from the words written by the author's pen allowed them to experience a scene more vividly in their imaginations. Reading was a great pastime. Parents read to their children, igniting their minds to visit far-off places artfully written about by the author. Adults read with pleasure and anticipation as they became involved in the plot of a story. Many evenings were spent sitting by the fireside with families embracing the joy of reading.

Life is faster paced now. Something must draw the reader into the book immediately, and detailed prologues will not achieve that. Also, people do not have the time to read as in the past, so many people prefer shorter books. Even so, some classic stories will never lose their appeal and will continue to be read for generations to come because of their uniqueness and creativity. We can learn from their techniques—classics will always be engaging. The following are three classic authors who still maintain their popularity today.

J.R.R. TOLKIEN

What really happens is that the story-maker proves a successful "sub-creator." He makes a Secondary World which your mind can enter. Inside it, what he relates is "true": It accords with the laws of that world. You therefore believe it, while you are, as it were, inside. The moment disbelief arises, the spell is broken; the magic, or rather art, has failed. You are then out in the Primary World again, looking at the little abortive Secondary World from outside.

~J.R.R. Tolkien

Tolkien's trilogy, *The Lord of the Rings* and *The Hobbit,* are examples of classic fantasy fiction which went to a whole new level in that genre. In these famous books, Tolkien made Middle Earth real—where humans, elves, dwarfs, orcs, ringwraiths, goblins, hobbits, wizards, and

ents lived. His trilogy expanded over centuries of history. He invented languages for different characters in his epic fantasy and gave attention to detail in plots, settings, and creatures, making Middle Earth even more vivid to readers. Some of his characters have whimsical names like Frodo Baggins, who has furry feet and is smaller than a dwarf, while others have names that distinctly sound evil, such as the dark Lord Sauron who made the Ring of Power—"one ring to rule them all." Tolkien was a master in the study of letter sounds and syllables, enabling him to create fitting names for his characters.

The Lord of the Rings trilogy was made into three major motion pictures (2001-2003), bringing the genius of Tolkien's epic tales to life and prompting a new surge of popularity to his books. His masterpiece trilogy took him eleven years to write, and the genius of his writing still remains amazing today.

C.S. LEWIS

Even in literature and art, no man who bothers about originality will ever be original: whereas if you simply try to tell the truth (without caring two-pence how often it has been told before) you will, nine times out of ten, become original without ever having noticed it.

~ C. S. Lewis

C.S. Lewis' vibrant imagination began as a child, and when he was grown, he wrote from that place of imagery. Lewis said this: "I wrote the books I should have liked to read if only I could have got them. That's always been my reason for writing. People won't write the books I want, so I have to do it for myself." A writer who enjoys a certain genre of writing will usually have passion to write in that genre. What excites the writer will excite the reader if the right words are used.

C.S. Lewis published more than thirty magnificent books, including poetry, science fiction, fantasy, and books defending the Christian faith. Through his perception, he could write so anyone could understand, going directly to the heart of the matter.

Recently, I read a book titled, *C.S. Lewis, Letters to Children.* This book is an accumulation of some of the many letters that C.S. Lewis received from children. Every morning he would sit down for an hour or more and personally respond to each letter in longhand. No question was too small for an answer. Among the many letters he received, thousands were from young fans of his most popular seven-book series, *The Chronicles of Narnia.* As I read through some of those letters and answers, I discovered much about the heart of C.S. Lewis. He once said, "I believe in Christianity as I believe that the sun has risen: not only because I see it, but because by it I see everything else." When he became a Christian, his passion was ignited not only in life but in his writing.

C.S. Lewis' creativity in writing is timeless. *The Chronicles of Narnia* are loved by so many people that three of his books in that series have now been made into full-length major motion pictures—*The Lion, the Witch, and the Wardrobe, Prince Caspian,* and *The Voyage of the Dawn Treader,* with more to come. His writing, and now motion pictures, will continue to be treasured by all ages.

JANE AUSTEN

I begin already to weigh my words and sentences more than I did, and am looking about for a sentiment, an illustration, or a metaphor in every corner of the room. Could my ideas flow as fast as the rain in the store closet, it would be charming.

~Jane Austen

Jane Austen's witty writings, which are more than two hundred years old, are timeless. Though Jane Austen never married, she was zealous about the quest for true love. The subject of love is universal—everyone wants to love and be loved. She wrote so people could experience love through unforgettable characters, which will always be a welcome read. One of her most popular books, *Pride and Prejudice,* is a complicated but endearing and intriguing love story. C. S. Lewis evidently enjoyed Jane Austen's work because he said, "I've been reading *Pride and Prejudice* on and off all my life and it doesn't wear out a bit."[1]

In the last twenty years, all of Jane Austen's six published books have been made into films and many several times over. Jane Austen, C.S. Lewis, J.R.R. Tolkien, as well as other classic writers, were able to write with the appeal that transcends time, which is a remarkable gift.

WRITING TODAY

Books that have sold well did so because they were innovative and diverse. If we write what is popular now, by the time it is published, some other type of writing may be more popular. Writing from old ideas produces, at best, watered-down text. New is only new once, and then it becomes old. Copycat writers are many, and that type of writing will become forgettable. Do not be guided by what is selling well. Be guided by your heart and passion for what you are writing— that is when originality will happen.

Because young people are not reading as much as they did in past years and are gravitating toward movies, television, MP3 players, computer games, and so on, writing must be exceptional to draw them to read. Never before have movies and television had such a pull on people. Television shows and movies are becoming so increasingly

1 Lyle W. Dorsett and Marjorie Lamp Mead, *C.S. Lewis, Letters to Children.* Touchstone, New York, 1985, pg. 37.

dramatic that viewers expect one exciting scene after another, and they get it. Producers today know that this is the only way to draw and keep viewers, so the bar keeps getting raised higher and higher with intensity.

To attract readers, books today must be fast-paced and exciting, just like movies. Writing should be thrilling and inspiring enough to persuade those who could be doing something they feel is more entertaining, to want to read instead. Reading a good book can be just as thrilling as watching an exciting movie, and in many ways more so, because the imagination is involved in the building of the plot and scenes. As a writer, you have the opportunity to give readers an amazing and enjoyable adventure in a novel and an unforgettable, inspiring experience in other genres. Reading should not become something of the past; creative writing can draw people back to the sheer joy of reading.

I find television very educating. Every time somebody turns on the set, I go into the other room and read a book.

~Groucho Marx
Comedian, actor

THE WRITING PROFESSION

Writing can be one of the most fulfilling and exciting types of work that you will ever do. If you write something of significance, not only will it bring enjoyment, hope, and inspiration to your readers now, but long after you have passed away, your legacy will live on through future readers. Benjamin Franklin, writer, politician, and one of the Founding Fathers of the United States once said the following:

If you would not be forgotten . . . either write things worth reading or do things worth writing.

— Chapter Three —
Ten Ways to Grow as a Writer

I write when I'm inspired, and I see to it that I'm inspired at nine o'clock every morning.

~Peter De Vries
American comic, visionary, and novelist

Whether you are an aspiring or seasoned writer, the following practical suggestions will help you grow as a writer.

1) Practice Writing

By running daily, muscles become stronger, so when it is necessary to run a long distance, a runner will have the strength and endurance to do it. We cannot expect to run a mile fast if we have not been building strength by running daily. The same is true of writing. The skill of writing well does not come overnight. First writings may look simple, almost elementary, but by practicing writing daily, new areas of skill and creativity will begin to develop. Daily contact with writing also keeps the veins of creativity open and flowing from the writer's pen. When I first began writing, it sometimes would take me several weeks to finish an article. Now, because of many years of practice, words flow better and faster.

If you do not feel you have the skills to write but greatly desire to write, start by writing something. Write emails and edit them to see if you can make them more exciting and readable. Write in a journal, and then edit that writing by pruning words in sentences to express the strongest elements of power and clarity. Before beginning the major goal of writing a book, set the goal of writing an article. When an article is accomplished, write more articles. The more you write, the more you will know what to write and the better it will become.

By consistently practicing writing, thought processes will begin to grow, and eventually finding the right words will come more easily. Robert Louis Stevenson once said, "The difficulty of literature is not to write, but to write what you mean to say." A writer must find the right words to represent his or her thoughts. With practice and perseverance it can be done. Practice communicating exactly what you mean to write until you are more than satisfied. The practice of writing concisely will produce articulate writing. As a bonus, aspiring writers will begin to develop a particular style—something unique that sets them apart from others. By being faithful to practice in the craft of writing, one day that amazing manuscript will come to life and be finished. Richard Bach said this wisely: "A professional writer is an amateur who didn't quit."

Don't say you don't have enough time. You have exactly the same number of hours per day that were given to Helen Keller, Pasteur, Michelangelo, Mother Teresa, Leonardo da Vinci, Thomas Jefferson, and Albert Einstein.

~H. Jackson Brown, Jr.
New York Times best-selling author

2) USE WORDS ELOQUENTLY

Like stones, words are laborious and unforgiving, and the fitting of them together, like the fitting of stones, demands great patience and strength of purpose and particular skill.

~Edmund Morrison,
Presidential Biographer

Writing eloquently is an obvious skill, but it is the most important one a writer can possess and determines the failure or success of every writer. A writer should be a wordsmith, using the English language (or any language) in a way that will achieve the greatest effect and the least clutter, yet be comprehendible, attention-grabbing, and ignited with passion.

Words are powerful. Strategically used, words can guide those reading them on a path of enlightenment and truth, dispelling darkness and defeat. Words can change circumstances and lives. The responsibility of using words to their most powerful and targeting effect should not be taken lightly.

With too many words, the meaning can get lost in the mumbo-jumbo of writing. Using excess words and trying to pound something into a reader's head is not an enjoyable experience for the reader. Readers should not have to work to understand the words written. Fewer, more powerful and eloquent words leave a positive and insightful memory. Use words to enlighten. Clear writing is concise writing.

WHEN WORDS HIT THEIR MARK

Some words create poetic sentences, perfectly fitting into something pleasing and deep. The following is an example of that type of sentence from the book, *The Handmaid and the Carpenter*, by Elisabeth Berg, a *New York Times* best-selling author.

There was a sad gaiety in the sound: the excitement of a journey tempered by the reason for it.[2]

In the story, Mary (Jesus' mother to be), was leaving to visit her beloved cousin, Elisabeth. "Sad gaiety," an oxymoron (two contradictory words used for effect), is brilliantly used to explain Mary's thoughts about the journey. As the sentence continues, "the excitement of a journey tempered by the reason for it," the reader understands that Mary's journey to Elisabeth's has always been and is still exiting, but the reason for it makes her sad. The words make their mark superbly.

Using literary devices such as an oxymoron or metaphor are the most effective when used sparingly. If these are overused, they will lose their power. Be selective with words and choose how to use them creatively and effectively. Every word should have meaning, but it will take time and effort to write that way. Words that are chosen carefully allow readers to feel just what they are supposed to feel—sometimes even beyond what the author intended. That is the power of words.

Jane Austen said: "An artist cannot do anything slovenly." We have all read lazy writing—words that fall flat with no life in them. Lazy writing, for example, is using words such as "very," "so," and "really" rather than finding the words that create a vivid picture.

Words are the most powerful force on the earth. You can make a difference in the life of those reading your words. When you leave this earth, knowing that your writing was published, what do you want to leave behind? Think about your goals and proceed accordingly.

2 Elisabeth Berg, *The Handmaid and the Carpenter,* Random House, New York, 2006, pg. 59.

3) BECOME MORE PASSIONATE

Write while the heat is in you. The writer who postpones the recording of his thoughts uses an iron which has cooled to burn a hole with. He cannot inflame the minds of his audience.

~Henry David Thoreau
American novelist and naturalist

When it feels like something is bursting to come forth, passion is strong and it is time to write. Passion in writing is having the enthusiasm to put into words what the heart is saying. Writing what comes from the heart cannot be forced into existence; it must come from inspiration and the right timing. Words written from inspiration deep within the writer are powerful tools. When the passion of the writer ignites the passion of the reader, it will leave a lasting mark on the reader.

Passion for what must be written should be the inspiration and starting point of all writing. F. Scott Fitzgerald, an American writer, said this well: "You don't write because you want to say something, you write because you have got something to say."

Whether you are a journalist, fiction or non-fiction writer, screen-writer, songwriter, or poet, passion should be the power behind your words. Passion is what ignites the fire in your words. Ralph Waldo Emerson said, "What lies behind us and what lies before us are tiny matters compared to what lies within us." Passionate writers dig deep to find those treasures within. Once passion is found, no rock will be left unturned until all is revealed and written from the depths of the writer's heart. The passion and commitment to write those treasures is what keeps the author writing until it is finished.

Passionate writers search for their own uniqueness and then write through the genre that best expresses their creativity. Genre comes from a French word meaning "kind" or "type." If you are now a fiction writer, at some time in your writing career you may begin to feel inspired to write a non-fiction book. Do it. Most important is to write in the area where you are inspired at the time you are writing.

You are unique, and only you can share what is most important in your heart. What brings the most passion and inspiration to your writing? Make a list of the things you love—you will likely find passion in those places. As you explore those areas, passion will grow.

Have you ever read a book that was immediately inspirational and you could not put it down? The passion of that writer for the subject ignited the passion within you, and you became intensely enthusiastic over what was written. The author achieved his or her purpose. When we read books from authors who are passionate and inspired about what they are writing, that writing will stay with us like no other. The words will actually become part of who we are.

The Lion, the Witch, and the Wardrobe, a book in *The Chronicles of Narnia* series, was not well-received at first by C.S. Lewis' publisher and some of his friends from his literary group called "The Inklings." They tried to persuade Lewis to not publish it—that it would ruin his career. His friend, J.R.R. Tolkien, criticized his book, saying too many elements clashed—talking animals and children, Father Christmas and an evil witch. C.S. Lewis did not listen. He knew his book needed to be published because he had great passion for what he had written. Tolkien was a genius in writing, but Lewis had to go with his heart, no matter what others said. Lewis' seven books were published and his series is still one of the most popular of all children's literature. Bottom line: You must follow your heart to find passion in your writing.

HINDRANCES TO BECOMING A PASSIONATE WRITER

Our passions are not too strong, they are too weak. We are far too easily pleased.

~C.S. Lewis

Some writers fall into the trap of comparing themselves to other writers, thinking that others write more eloquently, convincing themselves that their writing is mediocre or juvenile. Then they attempt to write like others by changing their unique style to mimic a writer who is successful. Readers can see through such writing.

Every writer has his or her own forte and creativity. Improve in writing techniques, but remain who you are—your voice and style. Once you find your own particular voice in writing, you will grow from that place every time you write. Readers will begin to recognize your writing.

If fame and fortune are the objectives of writing, then most definitely passion will be lost in writing. Seeking to become rich from writing could very well divert many into writing within areas they should not be writing. With aspiring writers and even seasoned writers, no guarantee exists that writing will be a money-making job, so making money should not be the incentive to write. Writing with passion brings great fulfillment to those who can savor that experience.

Passion in writing will deteriorate by writing to impress others. When writing to impress, what the writer may think is intelligently written usually conveys a tinge of arrogance in the article or book, giving the opposite effect of what was intended. One who writes like a "know-it-all" loses his or her likeability as an author.

C.S. Lewis wrote the following: "Never exaggerate. Never say more than you really mean."[3] Tell the truth in writing; do not extend it. Credibility is at stake if exaggeration is used. If readers are going to take the time to read something you have to say, they have to like and trust you and what you write. Write from a point of inspiration—your perspective ignited by passion will make your words the most effective.

In art, the hand can never execute anything higher than the heart can imagine.

~Ralph Waldo Emerson
American essayist, novelist, and poet

4) OBSERVE AND EXPERIENCE LIFE

A writer is an explorer. Every step is an advance into a new land.

~Ralph Waldo Emerson

Writers need the skill of observation—the ability to notice details to later use in writing. While observing, think about creative ways to describe something taken for granted by most. You can bring life to writing by taking something that may be generally unnoticed by most and turn it into something which everyone finds fascinating. You control your words and how you use them. Through the skill of observation and finding meaningful words to describe what is seen, ordinary writing can become extraordinary writing—fresh, new, and different.

---

3 Lyle W. Dorsett and Marjorie Lamp Mead, *C.S. Lewis, Letters to Children.* Touchstone, New York, 1985, pg. 87.

If you need to write a character sketch, begin watching people. Watch movements, expressions, reactions, and tone of voice. Study people and write physical descriptions in a writing journal to use later. Writing those observations into your characters will make the characters seem real.

Observe surroundings. If you want to write about Charleston, South Carolina or use it in a setting, go there, study it, even live there for a time if possible. Every writer needs an angle, a place from which a point is made, which will come from personal observation, not an observation through someone else. Practice observing details by using the five senses and write down in a journal how a new place looks, smells, tastes, feels, and sounds. Later, if you choose to use that place in a book, you will have notes about what made it unique from your perspective, which will bring life to your writing.

Experience life. If you have experienced falling in love and then had your heart broken, you can write just how that feels. Perhaps you or someone you know overcame an addiction to drugs—writing about that experience will come straight from your heart.

You may also develop empathy through understanding people and situations beyond what you have experienced. Perhaps something traumatic happened to a close friend or family member of yours. You felt his or her pain and began to understand through that experience the emotions felt by your friend.

Live outside of the box. Observe and experience beyond what you know. Travel beyond your own small world and watch. Notice details and write them down. Write from your perception. When you write about something you have experienced, it will become real to the reader. You will find that your writing will become diverse, heartfelt, and believable.

5) ENHANCE IMAGINATION AND CREATIVITY

> *You cannot depend on your eyes when your imagination
> is out of focus.*
>
> ~Mark Twain
> American humorist, satirist, and lecturer

Imagination is one of the greatest assets a writer can possess. Within this sphere of imagination, original ideas will abound and creativity will convey a new edge to writing. Everyone can look at the same cloud and see something different. As a child, I loved to lie on the ground, staring at the clouds with a friend. We could spend hours trying to see something new and then point to and describe what we saw. Our perspectives were different so what we saw was different; yet when my friend pointed to a cloud that looked like an elephant, I could see that elephant. Likewise, imagination is different in each person, but once written others will connect with the writer's imagination through his or her perspective.

A creative idea can come at any time—day or night. When an idea or inspiration for writing comes, jot it down wherever you are—even if it is in the middle of the night. A recorder is helpful so the idea can be recorded and later written. Keep a writer's journal and pen with you at all times.

Sometimes dreams are a great source for a plot. The plot for my first book, *The Chosen Path,* came from a dream. I loved the plot so much that I added the story around it. You never know when or where a creative idea for a book will come.

Complaining can kill creativity. Don't believe it? Listen to people who complain and notice how they maximize problems and minimize creative solutions. By listening to someone complain long enough, irritability and negativity will follow. It has been said, "Thoughts are like birds; they will fly and get in your hair, but you don't have to let them nest." Immersing your mind in the negative side of life could dampen the fires of creativity. Make an intentional effort to discard negative thoughts.

Gratitude is a helpful creativity enhancer. There is much to be thankful for—if you are breathing, there is still time to fulfill your dreams. Every day is a gift from God. Keeping a positive attitude will increase creativity. Believe you can write the book that you have set out to do. Henry Ford once said: "Whether you think you can or whether you think you can't, you're right!" Believe in yourself. If it is in your heart to write, do it.

6) READ

If you don't have the time to read, you don't have the time or the tools to write.

~Stephen King
Best-selling author

When reading, learn to spot what makes a book engaging. Learn also what makes it ineffective. Whether a book is good or bad, reading other books will teach you how to improve your own writing. By studying the styles of different writers, you will learn when to use formal or informal writing and how to use different points of view. Study how writers add conflict, characters, dialogue, and other writing elements in different genres to later help with your own writing.

Reading gives inspiration and ideas, which keeps you updated. By reading different subjects, your perspectives on subjects will broaden with new knowledge. Reading brings inspiration, and many writers are stimulated to find new angles on a topic, which later may be incorporated in writing a book.

Reading invigorates the mind and helps it to stay sharp. Reading not only stimulates creativity, but learning will reach a whole new level. Reading also increases vocabulary, adding depth for later use in writing. Reading brings great pleasure to those who take the time to savor the words.

Many of the books we read in our youth touched us deeply, and we will remember those books as we grow older. What type of books did you enjoy reading while you were young? Do you still enjoy adventures or fantasy books? Try writing in that genre and see where it leads. You might be surprised how much inspiration and passion you will discover.

7) SET GOALS

Even if you are on the right track, you'll get run over if you just sit there!

~Will Rogers
Cowboy, comedian, humorist, social commentator, and actor

In writing, something usually needs to be overcome—whether it is writer's block, a scene that just is not right, not enough time to write, distractions, or excuses not to write. If you are having trouble writing, it may help to spend some time in silence. In quietness and peace, your mind will find a place of rest where creativity can flow. Thomas Edison once said that "the best thinking has been done in solitude." Writing is a type of reflection that must be done alone and in quiet, so avoid writing where areas of distraction happen. Some people like to go outside and experience the tranquility of nature to get inspired. Clear your mind. Pray. Afterward, see where your thoughts lead. Everyone has some point of inspiration that must be found to enhance creativity.

Goals must be set in writing or the writing project will not be finished. What is your goal in writing? What do you hope to accomplish? My overall goal for this book is to inspire aspiring or even seasoned writers to improve in writing skills while igniting passion and creativity in writing. To write this book, goals were set within each chapter from an outline of subjects and points that I wanted to cover.

All goals can be completed if broken down into small enough parts. Be sure to assign dates to those goals to stay on track with a schedule. Keep your goals in your mind as you write. Post them on the wall where you write to stay focused, and check each goal off as it is accomplished.

GOALS + FOCUS = COMPLETION

If you are dedicated to finishing a writing project, set the goal of writing daily; it will become part of your routine, and eventually the project will be finished. The joy of finally finishing a manuscript, after painstakingly working on it for months, even years, will quickly override the obstacles that it took to write it. When obstacles are overcome, the joy of victory is all the more sweeter. Helen Keller said: "The marvelous richness of human experience would lose something of rewarding joy if there were no limitations to overcome. The hilltop hour would not be half so wonderful if there were no dark valleys to traverse." In the end, writers will understand that in overcoming obstacles, valuable lessons were learned, enabling the completion of the book.

ONE MOUNTAIN AT A TIME

Obstacles are those frightful things you see when you take your eyes off your goal.

~Henry Ford
American founder of Ford Motor Company and inventor

My son, Matthew, recently hiked the Appalachian Trail. The Appalachian Trail is nearly 2,200 miles of mountain terrain in fourteen states along the east coat of the United States, beginning at Springer Mountain, Georgia and ending at Mount Katahdin, Maine. Yearly, several thousand people attempt to hike the entire trail and less than 15 percent will actually achieve their goal. Within the first twenty to thirty miles, an average of 20 percent stop hiking. By the time many hikers reach North Carolina, another 50 percent drop out, and by West Virginia, 75 percent have stopped. From what I have read about hiking the Appalachian Trail, it is not the physical difficulties that stop people as much as the mental difficulties. Matthew confirmed this.

Matthew said that the first three days of hiking in the Georgia Mountains were the most difficult of his trip. The trail was straight up and down, no switchbacks, unlike most of the other trails on the mountains. His feet had become so blistered that he could hardly walk, and the energy he needed for hiking was being swallowed up by discouragement. He knew he had to do something, or he was going to stop. He said the only way he overcame his discouragement was to stay focused on the mountain that he was currently hiking—if he could just hike over that mountain without stopping and meet that goal, he could then look toward hiking the next mountain. Though he knew his overall goal was to hike the whole trail, he turned that large goal into smaller goals—he hiked one mountain at a time. That was a wise decision. His body was so tired that he could only give enough determination to hike the mountain before him.

Matthew had a map with him so he could mark off every town he passed on the trail. He could then see his accomplishments visually. Applying that to writing, write down goals so that every time one is accomplished, you can mark it off and continue on to the next.

Once steady progress is being made, the writing project will not seem such a complicated task.

Writing is a noble objective, but it can be mentally grueling, discouraging, and overwhelming at times if we allow it. Goals must be set and then completed. Even if the goal for one day is to write one page, that is still one page closer to finishing the writing project. If goals are broken down small enough, added with focus and determination, the ultimate goal of finishing a book will be achieved. Peter Mayle, a British author, wisely said: "Best advice on writing I've ever received: Finish!" Do not stop until you have completed your writing project. To achieve the extraordinary in writing may be difficult, but that will make the victory more sweet in the end. The written word will be available for generations to come.

> *Give me a stock clerk with a goal and I'll give you a man who will make history. Give me a man with no goals and I'll give you a stock clerk.*
>
> ~J.C. Penney
> Founder of J.C. Penney department stores

8) STAY MOTIVATED

Edward Young, a seventeenth-century English poet, said this well: "Procrastination is the thief of time." The worst enemy of a writer is procrastination. Time does not stand still, so it must be used wisely.

Many people dream about writing a book but never do because they are not motivated enough to begin and then finish it. Those who determine to finish what they begin separate themselves from the dreamers, who want to write a great book but never seem to be able to do it. Dreaming and visualizing the writing and publication of a book are natural processes of writing, but a dream without action will always remain a dream. As General George S. Patton said, "A good plan today is better than a perfect plan tomorrow."

Everyone needs time away from writing to refocus. The problem with some is they refocus too long on other activities and do not return quickly enough to writing. Every writer faces mountains and valleys in writing such as writer's block and lack of ideas. Television, computer games, email, phone calls, and so on can be distractions in writing, so determine from the beginning not to be pulled into those traps during a writing time. The victory of overcoming those distractions adds triumph—a great motivating factor in writing.

To stay motivated, the finish line must remain in view. As stated previously, goals need to be set and completed. Set time aside daily to write—work out a routine and adhere to it. As you see the writing project moving forward, inspiration will increase for the project, giving the needed motivation to want to finish the project.

Leonardo Da Vinci once said: "I have been impressed with the urgency of doing. Knowing is not enough; we must apply. Being willing is not enough; we must do." Keeping the completion as the goal will be the motivating factor to finish a writing project. Remember your dream. Success is the satisfaction of completing what you set out to do. The more you accomplish, the more you will want to accomplish.

THE PLEASURE OF WORK

Solomon wrote about work in Ecclesiastes 2:24:

So I decided there is nothing better than to enjoy food and drink and *to find satisfaction in work*. Then I realized that these pleasures are from the hand of God (NLT).

Work, you might say—how can anyone enjoy work? The word *work* to many does not bring pleasant thoughts. Think about how fulfilling it is to complete a goal—the sense of satisfaction when the work is completed. If you think about writing as a time of enjoyment, your writing will reflect your attitude.

Thomas Edison, who is famous for inventing the light bulb, had 1,093 patents in his life, averaging an invention every two weeks of his working career. He said, "I find the greatest pleasure, and so my reward, in the work that precedes what the world calls success." Working was Thomas Edison's greatest pleasure. The work involved in my son's adventure of hiking the Appalachian Trail became a great pleasure to him. I know this to be true in my own life when I am working toward finishing a goal such as a book. Yes, it takes effort and hard work to write, but pleasure can come in the midst of it. Samuel Johnson said: "What is written without effort is generally read without pleasure."

Enjoy the satisfaction of completing a project because it is a grand accomplishment, but do not stop there. As soon as you have finished one writing project, begin another. Stay motivated.

9) BE WILLING TO GROW

He who moves not forward, goes backward.

~Johann Wolfgang von Goethe
German playwright, poet, novelist

Creativity does not stay in a box. To grow in the writing craft, be willing to change old thoughts and adhere to new. If feasible, take a creative writing class or any writing class. Even a grammar class will help in reviewing and learning new skills. These classes will force you to practice and grow in the craft of writing. Writing is changing with the times, so it is important to keep up.

If you cannot take classes in writing, read and study books on the craft. Books on writing that are specific to a genre have a wealth of ideas about how to grow in your preferred area. Many have writing exercises that will help you to develop and grow creatively.

Allow your writing to expand in any way possible. You might try getting a job or interning at a publishing company. Connections in the writing field can help you get published. You will also gain much experience in the publishing field. Attend writers' conferences and learn new tips for writing. Practice writing what you learn. Writers' conferences also are helpful for learning how to get a book published through new contacts met in the publishing field.

Make it a goal to meet other writers and form a study group if possible. This is a great way to have others critique your writing. Try trading thoughts and points of inspiration. Once an established relationship with another writer is made, consider critiquing each other's work. Willingness to change and grow in writing will enable new growth in skills.

10) STAY ORGANIZED

First comes thought; then organization of that thought into ideas and plans; then transformation of those plans into reality. The beginning, as you will observe, is your imagination.

~Napoleon Hill
American author

Napoleon Hill, one of the earliest writers in "success" literature, was also famous for this quote: "What the mind of man can conceive, it can achieve." He knew that the importance of success was closely related to making plans and then utilizing those plans by organization.

Organization facilitates the writing process. William Zinsser in his book, *On Writing Well*, wrote: "Good writing is using the language in a way that will achieve the greatest strength and the least clutter. Clear thinking becomes clear writing. It is impossible for a muddy thinker to write good English." Our minds are less cluttered if less clutter is around where we write. My suggestion is to have a clean desk or area where the writing takes place. Some writers work in a mound of papers, which can bring confusion to any project. Perhaps in the huge mound, an idea for a book is within that pile—much time could be wasted trying to find it. If the writing area is organized, that type of frustration will not happen.

Organize ideas for an article or book. I put my ideas in the appropriate folder for each project on my computer. I recommend having a small filing cabinet to keep any hard copies of ideas in separate folders per project so they will be organized and easily found. Two times I have lost partial books on my computer when one computer died and another was stolen. I have learned the difficult way to keep copies of manuscripts. An easy way to keep updated writing is to email the writing to yourself daily or keep an updated CD or flashdisk. That way the latest version will always be available.

Free your mind so you can think clearly. If you have something pressing that needs to be done, do it. On the other hand, do not let things that are unnecessary keep you from writing. Anything and everything will become a distraction if you let it. In quietness and peace, your mind will find a place of rest, becoming clear of stress and problems. In this place, creativity can begin to flow.

Stretching yourself as a writer is the only way to grow in the craft. Writing skills sharpen as they are used. Be yourself when you write. Who knows what great things are yet to come in your writing?

A writer is dear and necessary for us only in the measure of which he reveals to us the inner workings of his very soul.

~Count Leo Tolstoy
Russian novelist

CHAPTER FOUR

THE BASICS
OF GRAMMAR

I never made a mistake in grammar but one in my life and as soon as I done it I seen it.

~ Carl Sandburg
Pulitzer Prize winner, poet, and biographer

A strong foundation and framework must exist for any building to stand. If the foundation and framework are poorly built, the building will eventually crack and even fall. Likewise, a writer must have a strong foundation in grammar skills for the framework, the writing, to stand. If a book is poorly written, no matter how insightful and passionate the theme, the writing will fall flat. For that reason, understanding the basics of grammar is crucial. A writer who becomes knowledgeable and skilled with grammar skills is like a craftsman who is skilled with his tools.

PARTS OF SPEECH

Understanding the role of each part of speech will give a strong framework for grammar, which in turn will strengthen writing. The following is an overview of the eight parts of speech: nouns, verbs, pronouns, adjectives, adverbs, prepositions, conjunctions, interjections, and articles (though articles are not considered a part of speech, they are frequently used).

NOUNS

A noun refers to a person, place, or thing, but a noun can also refer to an idea or something abstract. A noun will usually have several roles in a sentence—the subject or direct or indirect object of the subject.

Different types of nouns used are proper, concrete, abstract, and collective nouns.

- **Proper nouns** are indicated by a capital letter and include individuals, events, places, or things: Moravian Falls, Harry, December.

- **Concrete nouns** are tangible: cat, house, book, nectarine.

- **Abstract nouns** describe qualities, ideas, or feelings: love, joy, imagination, justice, bravery.

- **Collective nouns** refer to a group of things, people, or concepts: family, cattle, class, crew.

Four basic properties of nouns include: gender, person, number, and case.

- **Gender:** indicates the sex of the noun.
  Masculine: uncle, boy, king
  Feminine: aunt, girl, queen
  Common: sibling, parent, dog, tree

- **Person:** the relationship between the noun and the subject (shows where or when a person is speaking, being spoken to, or being spoken about). For further understanding on first, second, and third person, see pages 138-139.

First person: I am here.
Second person: You are here.
Third person: She is here.

- **Number:** one or more nouns
  Singular: one noun—horse
  Plural: more than one noun—horses

- **Case:** grammatical function of the noun (noun's relationship to other words in the sentence).
  Nominative—doer of the action is the noun: A **thinker** ponders.
  Objective—the noun receives the action or object of preposition: Duchess barked at the **cat.**
  Possessive—noun ownership: **Sally's** car is a hybrid.

SUBJECT AND PREDICATE

Every complete sentence must have a subject and predicate or it is an incomplete sentence or fragment. A fragment cannot stand alone. It poses as a sentence but is not one. The following examples are fragments: the swift stream; beyond the dunes.

The subject is what or who the sentence is about, while the predicate is the action (verb) that happens in the sentence.

- The dog played with the cat. Two nouns (dog and cat) are in this sentence, so how is the subject determined? First, isolate the verb (played). To find the subject, ask: Who played with the cat? The dog played with the cat, so **dog** is the subject. Cat is the object of the subject, dog.

- **Hint:** A subject can never be in a prepositional phrase. This will be reviewed later in this chapter.

VERBS

A verb is the heart of the sentence. A verb serves as the critical element of the predicate in a sentence, which indicates an action, state of being, or event to the subject. Recognizing a verb is the most important part of understanding a sentence. A verb or compound verb (two or more verbs) must be in every sentence for it to be complete.

- Matthew hiked the Appalachian Trail. **Hiked** is the verb.

- In December, snow will fall before Christmas. **Will fall** is the compound verb.

Verbs can change their form unlike other parts of speech. For example, walk can become walks, walked, or walking, depending on the tense. A verb can also change to a different form of that word such as sit and sat.

TRANSITIVE AND INTRANSITIVE VERBS

A transitive verb expresses an action, such as eat, walk, climb, write, and it must have a direct object (someone or something that receives the action). Direct objects can be nouns, pronouns, clauses, or phrases. Review the following sentence:

- Mary **recycles** plastic, glass, and aluminum. Mary is the subject. Recycles is the transitive verb. What does Mary recycle? **Plastic, glass**, and **aluminum** are the direct objects.

- The verb is intransitive when no direct object follows an action verb such as the following: Mary **recycles.**

HELPING VERBS

Some types of verbs help the action, so they are called "helping verbs." Helping verbs help clarify when the action will take place.

The most common helping verbs are the following: *am, is, are, can, do, did, was, were, could, should, would, have, had, has, been, shall, will,* and *might.*

- Amber **did come** to the youth rally. **Did** is the helping verb; **come** is the verb; together the verbs form a compound verb.

BASIC VERB TENSES

Three basic verb tenses occur in English: past, present, and future. Each verb tense has a perfect form, progressive form, and perfect progressive form. The perfect form is when the action is completed. The progressive form is ongoing action. The perfect progressive form is when the ongoing action will be finished at a specific time. Further explanation follows.

PAST, PRESENT, AND FUTURE TENSES OF VERBS

An important aspect of understanding verbs is their relationship to time. Verbs tell if something has happened, is happening now, or will happen. An event that has happened is in the past tense, and no helping verb is needed. To form the past tenses of regular forms of verbs, simply add *-d* or *-ed.* An event that is happening now and something that is always true or has unchanging action is in the present tense. An event that will happen later is in the future tense. In a regular form, *will* is added to the future tense of the verb.

Regular forms of verbs are the simplest to understand.

- Present: I **bake** bread every day.

- Past: I **baked** bread yesterday.

- Future: I **will bake** bread tomorrow.

Examples of Regular Forms of Verbs

Present	Past	Future
laugh	laughed	will laugh
talk	talked	will talk
hike	hiked	will hike

In irregular forms, the verb in the past tense is a different or irregular form of the word. See examples below.

- Present: I **grow** vegetables in the summer.
- Past: I **grew** vegetables last summer.
- Future: I **will grow** vegetables next summer.

Examples of Simple Irregular Forms of Verbs

Present	Past	Future
sit	sat	will sit
speak	spoke	will speak
draw	drew	will draw

Now that we have established present, past, and future verbs, let's move on to two more types of tenses and modifications from which verbs are formed. In the present and past participle, one or more helping verbs must be used with the verb. The past participle means that something started in the past. One easy way to remember the present particle is that it is formed by adding -*ing* to the verb.

- Present: I **drive** to work every day.
- Past: I **drove** to work yesterday.
- Past participle: I **have driven** to work for years.
- Present participle: I **will be driving** to work for many more years.

Principal Parts of Irregular Verbs with Examples

Present	Past	Past Participle	Present Participle
am, is, are	was, were	been	being
break	broke	broken	breaking
come	came	come	coming
do	did	done	doing
eat	ate	eaten	eating
see	saw	seen	seeing
tell	told	told	telling
wear	wore	worn	wearing
write	wrote	written	writing

If you are unsure of what form to use with the verb, the principal parts of irregular verbs are found in a dictionary. If it is not shown in the dictionary, then it is a regular verb as indicated in the first chart.

PROGRESSIVE VERB FORMS

Present Progressive Tense

Present progressive tense means an ongoing or progressive action is occurring. The verb action is happening at the time the sentence is being written. *Am, is,* or *are* is used with a verb that ends in *-ing.* Review the following sentences.

- Present tense: I **walk**.
- Present progressive tense: I **am walking**.

Past Progressive Tense

Past progressive tense describes a past action that is in progress when another action happened in the past. *Was* or *were* is used with a verb that ends in *-ing.*

- I **was walking**.

Future Progressive Tense

Future progressive tense describes an ongoing or progressive action that will happen in the future. *Will be* or *shall be* is used with a verb that ends in *-ing.*

- I **will be walking.**

PERFECT VERB TENSES

Though it may seem difficult to understand at first, different verb forms will begin to make sense as you think about the structure of the sentence. Three parts to the past participle are present, past, and perfect tense.

Present perfect tense means that the action was completed or is continuing up to the present time. The verb is considered present tense because it was finished or is still true in the present. *Have* (present tense) is used with the past participle of the verb to form the present perfect tense.

- I **have walked.**

Past perfect tense means action that was completed in the past (an action that took place before another past action). Unlike the present perfect tense, both verbs are in the past. *Had* (past tense) is used with the past participle of the verb to form the past perfect tense.

- We **had walked** ten miles by Saturday.

Future perfect tense means the action or state will be completed before a certain time in the future. It may not have happened but it will happen. *Will have* must be used with the past participle of the verb.

- We **will have walked** ten miles before Saturday.

PERFECT PROGRESSIVE TENSES

The past perfect tense also has a progressive form. This tense is indicated by the form of a helping verb. Dynamic verbs (verbs showing qualities that are capable of change) are used in progressive tenses. The following is a brief overview.

Present perfect progressive describes an event or action which started in the past and is still happening, and it may continue into the future. *Has/have been* and the present participle of the verb (verb ending in -*ing*) are used to form present perfect progressive.

- We **have been walking** since Monday.

Past perfect progressive describes an ongoing event or action that took place before another past event. *Had been* and the present perfect tense of the verb (verb ending in -*ing*) are used to form the past perfect progressive.

- We **had been walking** for days, but on Saturday we reached our goal.

Future perfect progressive describes an event that will happen by a particular future time. *Will have been* and the present participle of the verb (verb ending in -*ing*) are used to form future perfect progressive.

- By Saturday, we **will have been walking** for six days.

VERB CONSISTENCY

Always check for verb tense consistency in all sentences. Typically, there should not be a shift among past, present, and future tenses within a sentence or paragraph.

The Bible and some other books speak in the present: (Jesus *tells* us to love one another) even though it happened in the past. This is acceptable. In general, people from the past should be quoted or described as speaking in past terms: they wrote, they said, they warned.

VERB AND SUBJECT AGREEMENT

Agreement indicates that the verb changes depending on the type of noun to which it refers. The verb and subject should agree in number. If the noun is singular, the verb should be singular. If the noun is plural, the verb should be plural. To check for subject and verb agreement, you must identify the subject of the sentence.

Simple rule: To determine the subject, exclude all words in a prepositional phrase (a list of common prepositions is listed on page 67.

Review the following sentence: The dog was in his house. *In his house* is a prepositional phrase, so we know that house is not the subject. Who is in the house? Dog. The verb is *was*. We can conclude that since the subject is singular (**dog**), then the verb must be singular as well (**was**).

One exception: When using **you**, even if it is used in a singular form, the verb is plural when used after **you**: You *have been* a great comfort to him (have been is plural).

A few other exceptions to the simple rule occur, so when in doubt, consult a grammar reference manual for all questions concerning nouns and verbs.

SPLIT INFINITIVE

An infinitive consists of the preposition *to* and the base form of the verb. A split infinitive is when a word is placed between *to* and the verb. In formal writing, split infinitives should be avoided. When the sentence construction becomes awkward, they should also be avoided. The following are examples of infinitives, split infinitives, and corrections.

Infinitives	Split Infinitives	Corrected
to go	to boldly go	to go boldly *or* boldly to go
to want	to always want	to want always *or* always to want
to buy	to quickly buy	to buy quickly or quickly to buy

VERBS—PASSIVE AND ACTIVE

As stated, a verb describes the action in a sentence. Two types of verbs are passive and active. If the subject receives the action (not doing the action) of the verb, the verb is passive. Passive verbs include using a form of the *be* verb: *are, am, is, was, were, are,* or *been.*

Using active verbs gives more direct, forceful, and concise sentences. However, if the active voice is always used, writing can become too dramatic. Passive voice can add variety at times in narratives. Trust your judgment. Which sentence sounds better in the context in which you are writing? That is the answer to using a passive or active verb.

- The beached whale **was saved** by the environmentalists. *Whale* (received the action) is the subject; *was saved* is the passive verb, which weakens the sentence.

- Review the rewritten sentence with an active verb: The environmentalists **saved** the beached whale. The sentence was shortened by two words and is stronger and more concise.

Passive verbs can make a sentence awkward.

- The brakes **were slammed** on by Ed as his bike sped downhill.

Active verbs make the sentence stronger and more concise.

- Ed **slammed** on the brakes as his bike sped downhill.

Other Examples:

- Passive verb: The man **was kicked** by the donkey.
- Active verb: The donkey **kicked** the man.

- Passive verb: My first cat **will be** always remembered by me.
- Active verb: I **will** always remember my first cat.

PRONOUNS

Pronouns take the place of specific people, places, things, and ideas and are often used to replace a noun if that noun is understood in a sentence.

Common Pronouns

I	me	you	he	him	she
her	we	they	them	us	it

Pronouns make writing more interesting by allowing the writer to not use the same noun repeatedly. However, a problem can occur if the replacement pronoun is not clear. Review the following sentences:

Sarah and Mary were walking to the sea turtle hospital at Topsail Beach. On the way to the hospital, **they** met Theresa, **their** friend. **She** said, "Will **you** come with us?"

- they—refers to Sarah and Mary
- their—refers to Sarah and Mary
- She—not clear. She could refer to Sarah or Mary, even Theresa.
- you—not clear—do not know who "you" is

Since **she** is not clear, the proper noun should be used for clarity. **You** is not clear so the proper noun should be specified as well.

- **Corrected sentence:** Sarah and Mary were walking to the sea turtle hospital at Topsail Beach. On the way to the hospital, they met their friend, Theresa. Mary said, "Will you come with us?"

SINGULAR AND PLURAL PRONOUNS

Examples of singular pronouns are the following: *anyone, each, nobody, another, someone,* and *something.* Examples of plural pronouns are the following: *both, few, many,* and *others.*

PRONOUN AGREEMENT

A pronoun needs to agree with the word it stands for (in number, person, and gender). One of the most common grammatical errors in a sentence occurs when pronouns are not in agreement. Typically, it helps to change the subject to plural as with the following:

- **Incorrect***:* When an *athlete* (singular) runs in a race, *they* (plural) will need much endurance training.

- **Correct***:* When *athletes* (plural) run in a race, *they* (plural) will need much endurance training.

COMMON TYPES OF PRONOUNS

The following are some of the most common pronouns used in writing: personal, reflexive and intensive, indefinite, demonstrative, interrogative, and relative pronouns.

1. **Personal pronouns** are used as a substitute for the names of people or things that perform actions. They designate the person speaking, the person spoken to, or the person or thing being spoken about.

    - "A man who carries a cat by the tail learns something **he** can learn no other way."

    ~Mark Twain

53

a. **Subjective (nominative) pronouns** can only be used when the pronoun is the subject of the verb. Subjective pronouns include the following: *I, you, she, he, they, we, it*, and *who*.

- **She** will be going to the beach soon.
- **I** am recycling all aluminum.

b. **Objective pronouns** are used as the object of the verb or preposition. Objective pronouns include the following: *me, us, you, him, her, them, it*, and *whom*.

- Tim gave **me** a copy of the book, *Pride and Prejudice.*

c. **Possessive pronouns** are used to show possession before or after a noun: *my, mine, your, yours, his, her, hers, its, our, ours, their*, and *theirs*. This is the easiest pronoun to substitute. Do not use an apostrophe with possessive pronouns.

- **Her** dog is a terrier mix.

2. **Reflexive and intensive pronouns** are typically used when the object of a sentence is the same as the subject. These pronouns *always* refer to another noun or pronoun in the same sentence which represents the same person or persons. Reflexive and intensive pronouns include the following: *myself, yourself, himself, herself, itself, ourselves, yourselves*, and *themselves*.

Reflexive pronouns refer to the subject, directing the action of the verb back to the subject.

- Dana dressed **herself** in warm clothing for the outdoor party.

Intensive pronouns emphasize the subject of the sentence (another noun or pronoun) and do not function as the subject. They usually are placed near the subject.

- Intensive Pronoun: Dana **herself** is going to be starring in the theatrical production.

- Never use "myself" as a substitute for me or I.
  Incorrect: The banana was mashed and put in the batter by myself.
  Myself cannot be used because there is no other noun or pronoun in the sentence that refers to myself.

  Correct: The banana was mashed and put in the batter by me.
  Better: I mashed and put the banana in the batter **myself**. Myself can be used because it refers to I.

3. **Indefinite pronouns** are usually near the subject of the sentence and are words that replace nouns without specifying which noun they replace, conveying the idea of all, any, none, or some. A common mistake in grammar is when a singular pronoun is used with a plural verb such as the following example:

   - **Incorrect:** Each are going to see the movie, *The Voyage of the Dawn Treader*. *Each* is a singular pronoun which requires the singular verb *is*. The sentence should read:
     Correct: Each **is** going to see the movie, *The Voyage of the Dawn Treader*.

Singular Indefinite Pronouns

another	anybody	anyone	anything	each
either	everybody	everyone	everything	little
much	neither	nobody	no one	nothing
one	other	somebody	someone	something

- Give a concert ticket to **everyone**.

Plural Indefinite Pronouns

both	few	many	others	several

- Many have come but **few** will remain.

Singular or Plural Indefinite Pronouns

all	any	more	most	none	some

- **None** were found among the archives.

4. **Demonstrative pronouns** identify a noun or pronoun and stand for something that can be pointed to. The singular demonstrative pronouns are *this* and *that*. The plural pronouns are *these* and *those*.

   - **This** is a day to remember.
   - **Those** Scotch Bonnets are North Carolina's state sea shell.

5. **Interrogative pronouns** are used when asking questions. The interrogative pronouns include the following: *who, whom, which,* and *what*. The compounds are formed by adding *-ever: whoever, whomever, whichever,* and *whatever*.

   - **Who** is going to the zoo? **Whom** shall I say called?

6. **Relative pronouns** relate to other nouns that have preceded them in a sentence. They are used at the beginning of a subordinate clause to give more information about the main clause.

   Relative pronouns that refer to people are *who, whoever, whom,* and *whomever*.

- The candidate **who** wins this election will have a difficult job.

  Who is the subject of the verb "wins" and introduces the subordinate clause: "who wins this election."

a. Who and whoever (subjective case)

Who and *whoever* are subjects in the nominative pronoun form. *Who* and *whomever* are only used in reference to people. They also complete the meaning of linking verbs. A linking verb links two ideas. Use *who* and *whoever* whenever he, she, they, I, or we could be substituted in the clause. Again, *who* is always the subject of a verb. If you are in doubt, rearrange the clause as shown in the parenthesis.

- The one **who** is going is Janice (*who* is referring to one).

  Who is buying the diamond bracelet? *Who* is the subject and *is buying* is the verb. (*He* is buying the diamond bracelet.)

  Whoever wants to see the panda needs to be patient. *Whoever* is the subject and *wants* is the verb.

b. Whom and whomever (objective case)

Whom or *whomever* are used in the objective case (pronouns used as objects of verbs or prepositions). Use *whom* whenever him, her, them, me, or us could be substituted as the object of the verb or preposition in the *whom* clause. *Whom* and *whomever* are only used in reference to people. Rearrange the clause as needed.

- **Whom** will you invite to the movie? *Whom* is the object of the verb *will*. (You will invite *her* to the movie.)

- I will give the extra cookie to **whomever** you think deserves it. Whomever is the object of the preposition *to*. (You can give the extra cookie to *him*.)

c. **Who vs. whom**

If you have difficulty determining when to use *who* and *whom*, there is an easy way to determine which one to use. *Who* is a subject like *he*. *Whom* is an object like *him*. Test *who* and *whom* by substituting them in a sentence as follows.

- Who/whom is going to stop using plastic bags? (*He* is going to stop using plastic bags.)

  Correct: Who is going to stop using plastic bags?

- Who/whom will you do your project with? (You will be doing your project with him.) *Whom* is the object of the verb *will*.

  Correct: Whom will you do your project with?

Relative pronouns that refer to places, things, and ideas are *which* and *that*.

a. **Which**—use *which* when referring to a specific thing or place.
   - Which dog is yours?
   - Use *which* when a thing or place was previously mentioned (typically introduces nonessential clause).
   - Koalas, which live in Australia, only eat eucalyptus leaves.

b. **That**—use *that* when referring to a species, class, or type. *That* is typically used when introducing an essential clause.
   - This is the dog **that** was missing.

c. **That vs. which**

That and *which* are only used in reference to things and places, not people. Many writers interchangeably use *that* and *which*. However, there is a rule to help choose which one to use. *That* should be used with restrictive clauses and *which* with nonrestrictive clauses. Further explanation follows.

RESTRICTIVE (ESSENTIAL) CLAUSES

A restrictive clause restricts or limits the identity of a subject. A restrictive clause is essential to understanding the meaning of the sentence. When writing a restrictive clause, introduce it with the word *that* and no comma. Remember to use *who* when referring to a person. Review the following examples:

- The house **that** was on Maple Street was green.
- The girl **who** sat behind the desk was reading.

NONRESTRICTIVE (OR NONESSENTIAL) CLAUSES

A nonrestrictive clause tells something about a preceding subject, but it does not limit or restrict the meaning of that subject. Use *which* to introduce the nonrestrictive clause, and place a comma before *which*.

- The house, **which** is on Maple Street, is green.
  The nonrestrictive clause above tells us that the house is on Maple Street, but it does not tell us which particular house on Maple Street is green. There could be many green houses on Maple Street.

THE USE OF RESTRICTIVE AND NONRESTRICTIVE CLAUSES IN THE SAME SENTENCE

- The antique wagon **that** was in the playroom, **which** was purchased for $10 in 1934, was missing.

The restrictive clause beginning with *that* tells us there was only one antique wagon in the playroom and it was missing. There could be more antique wagons in the playroom, other than the one mentioned. The nonrestrictive clause beginning with *which* tells us that the owner paid $10 for it in 1934.

Again, use *that* to introduce a restrictive clause and *which* to introduce a nonrestrictive clause. However, it is becoming more common for writers to introduce an essential clause with *which,* especially when *that* has already been used once in the sentence. In that case, it is acceptable to use *which.*

- Lions **that** hunt in packs are more dangerous than tigers **which** travel alone.

MORE PROBLEMS WITH PRONOUN USAGE

1. General/broad reference

Read the following sentence and determine what *he* and *it* refers to.

- His friend is a doctor, but he is not interested in *it.*

He is not interested in *it.* Who is not interested in *it?* What is *it?* This sentence does not make sense. Also, *he* is not clarified and a pronoun must refer to the same form of the word in the sentence. A better way to write this sentence would be to use the proper noun for *his* and define *it.*

- Barry's friend is a doctor, but Leo is not interested in becoming a doctor.

The tendency might be to use *one* for the last "doctor" in the sentence, but in this sentence it still would not be clear (*one* could refer to friend or doctor).

2. Gender problems

Avoid using *his/her*; rather, use *his* or *her*, and if possible use *their* to avoid the masculine bias of *his*. The male form of a pronoun typically refers to a specific noun. Although grammatically correct, there can be a problem with this. Read the following example:

- On the first day of school, a teacher cannot remember all of the names of *his* students.

The sentence is actually referring to all teachers, not one. Some could interpret this sentence that all teachers are male, which is not the case. The following is one way to correct it, but it is awkward.

- On the first day of school, a teacher cannot remember all the names of *his* or *her* students.

Another way to solve this pronoun dilemma is to make the noun and pronoun plural.

- On the first day of school, *teachers* cannot remember all the names of *their* students.

Last, the sentence can be rewritten to include no pronouns. Sometimes this is the best way.

- Teachers cannot remember every student by name on the first day of school.

3. Pronoun consistency

Lack of consistency in pronoun structure in a sentence can be problematic. The following sentences illustrate inconsistency in agreement with the noun and pronoun.

- **Incorrect:** *We* want to stop using plastic bags at the store, but *you* don't know what else to use.
- **Correct:** *We* want to stop using plastic bags, but *we* don't know what else to use.

- **Incorrect:** *We* can buy string, hemp, or jute bags and use *it* instead of plastic.
- **Correct:** *We* can buy string, hemp, or jute bags and use *those* instead of plastic.

ADJECTIVES

Adjectives are used to describe nouns or pronouns, giving more information about them. They tell what kind, which one, and how many. They can modify a noun in a slight or considerable way. Adjectives are divided into two basic classes: descriptive and limiting.

Descriptive adjectives are used to describe a noun or pronoun.
- The **warm** weather was welcomed.
- Mark drove the **hybrid** car to the mountains.

Limiting adjectives are used to limit the meaning of a noun or pronoun. Limiting adjectives are used to clarify.
- She owns **two** dogs.
- **Some** restaurants are not open on Sunday.

Although adjectives help clarify nouns, typically they should be used sparingly. How do you like the following sentence?

- The cold, ever-flowing, silent wind pushed the dead, brown leaves against the blue-gray wall.

Not only is that sentence boring and annoying, but readers will get lost in the adjectives. Adjectives can be helpful at times, but if overused they can hinder writing. The goal of a writer should be for the reader to experience rather than be told.

COMPARATIVE AND SUPERLATIVE ADJECTIVES

Comparative adjectives are used to compare two or more people, places, or things. They are formed when adding *-er* to the end of the adjective or by using *more* or *less* before an adjective typically with two or more syllables. Do not use both.

- **Incorrect:** Ben is more taller than Sam.
- **Correct:** Ben is **taller** than Sam.

For comparative adjectives that have one syllable, add *-er:*

- **warm, warmer**

For comparative adjectives that end with *y,* change the *y* to *i* and add *-er.*

- **happy, happier**

Superlative adjectives are used to describe three or more items to the highest degree in comparison. They are never used with two items. Sometimes *most* or *least* are used to describe the comparison, but typically adding *-est* is the best choice. Do not use a superlative adjective ending in *-est* and *most* or *least* in the same sentence.

When superlative adjectives end in *e,* add *-st.*

- **blue, bluest**

Superlative adjectives that end with *y,* change the *y* to *i* and add *-est.*

- **wacky, wackiest**
- **Incorrect:** Flour, shortening, and buttermilk are used to make the most tastiest biscuits.
- **Correct:** Flour, shortening, and buttermilk are used to make the **tastiest** biscuits.

Mark Twain summarizes the subject of using adjectives admirably:

I notice that you use plain, simple language, short words and brief sentences. That is the way to write English—it is the modern way and the best way. Stick to it; don't let fluff and flowers and verbosity creep in. When you catch an adjective, kill it. No, I don't mean utterly, but kill most of them—then the rest will be valuable. They weaken when they are close together. They give strength when they are wide apart. An adjective habit, or a wordy, diffuse, flowery habit, once fastened upon a person, is as hard to get rid of as any other vice.

ADVERBS

Adverbs are qualifiers that describe verbs, adjectives, and other adverbs. Before we continue, let's compare a few examples of adjectives and adverbs to show the difference.

- adjective: a **fast** walker—**fast** (adjective) describes the noun, **walker**
- adverb: walks **fast**—**fast,** (adverb) describes the verb, **walks**

Typically, most words that end in *-ly* are adverbs, but there are a few exceptions that can be used as adverbs and adjectives such as: quarterly, yearly, early, only, weekly, and monthly.

Some recognizable prepositions can also be used as adverbs in verb phrases: in, out, up, on, and off.

- adverb: Put **on** a new shirt.
- preposition: A stain is **on** the new shirt.

Adverbs can show manner, place, time, frequency, and degree. The following are examples of each type.

- **Adverbs of manner** come after the direct object or if there is no direct object, after the verb:
  - Riley will **carefully** plant the flowers.

- **Adverbs of place** answer the question: Where? Usually this adverb is placed after the direct object or verb:
  - Duchess saw you **there**.
- **Adverbs of time** answer the question: When? Typically, this adverb comes at the beginning or end of the sentence:
  - **Before** we go to the park, let's get some bottled water.
- **Adverbs of frequency** answer the question: How many times?
  - Moses **always** comes when called.
- **Adverbs of degree** answer the question: To what extent? Usually this adverb modifies an adverb or adjective before the word it describes:
  - We are **almost** finished.

Using too many adverbs is a sign of laziness in the writer.

- Tom angrily put his glass down as he walked toward Mary.
- Better: Tom flung his glass against the wall as he edged closer to Mary.

Adverbs can weaken writing with redundant words. The following are examples of useless adverbs in sentences.

1. Cooperate together and finish the puzzle (cooperate means to work together). Delete *together*.

2. The radio blared loudly. (How else can a radio blare but loudly?) Delete *loudly*.

3. He clenched his teeth tightly. (There's no other way to clench teeth.) Delete *tightly*.

4. The horse galloped swiftly. (Do horses gallop slowly?) Delete *swiftly*.

5. The house was completely destroyed. (Destroyed means completely ruined.) Delete *completely*.

6. Follow after Mary, and she will lead you to the oasis. (After has the same meaning as follow in this sentence.) Delete *after*.

Adverbs: Very, So, Really

Three of the most overused adverbs are *really, so,* and *very.* These adverbs are frequently used by many writers to try and add more feeling/intensity to their writing. Often, the opposite occurs and the sentence weakens instead. With thought, a more suitable word can replace them, making the writing more powerful.

Consider these two sentences:
* It was a cold day.
* It was a very cold day.

Are you convinced that a very cold day is colder than a cold day? A cold day is still a cold day. Reflect upon the following sentence.

* It was a glacial day.

Better yet would be to add words so the reader can experience the coldness of the day:

* While skating, the girls trembled as thin slivers of ice hit their legs.

A picture is given, but the word cold was not used. Expressive words paint a picture for the reader.

Think about adverbs as pepper. Adverbs in writing, like pepper in cooking, add seasoning, but it is wise to be sparing with the use of both. Pepper can ruin food the same way adverbs can ruin writing.

Again and again in careless writing, strong verbs are weakened by redundant adverbs.[4]

~William Zinsser
Writer, editor, teacher

4 William Zinsser, *On Writing Well,* HarperCollins, New York, 2006, pg. 68.

PREPOSITIONS

A preposition shows the relation of nouns, verbs, and phrases in a sentence. The following is a common list of prepositions.

List of Common Prepositions

aboard	about	above	according to
across	after	against	along (with)
amid	among	around	at
back of	because of	before	behind
below	beneath	beside	between
beyond	but	by	concerning
contrary to	despite	down	during
except	for	from	in
inside	instead of	into	like
near	of	off	on
out	outside	over	past
rather than	regarding	since	through
throughout	till	to	together with
toward	under	underneath	until
unto	up	up to	upon
with	with regard to	within	without

Is the following a complete sentence? On the bike. *On* is the first word in the prepositional phrase, "on the bike." As stated, a subject is never in a prepositional phrase. Second, the following question cannot be answered: Who is on the bike? Again, this confirms there is no subject. Third, there must be a subject and a predicate in a sentence. No predicate (verb) is in this sentence. Conclusively, "on the bike" is a fragment and is not a complete sentence.

Ending Sentences with Prepositions

Writing has changed through the years and so have the rules. Whether the sentence ends with a preposition or not should depend on the emphasis and effect desired. Often there is a better way to end a sentence without using a preposition. However, trying to avoid ending a sentence with a preposition may lead to unnatural, awkward results, such as the following:

- Where did he come from? (natural)
- From where did he come? (awkward)

The following sentence was reportedly written by Winston Churchill. It is an ideal example of why a sentence *should* at times end with a preposition.

- This is the sort of English up with which I will not put.

The above sentence is confusing and awkward, yet it follows the rule that no sentence should end with a preposition.

The following is the sentence rewritten, ending with a necessary preposition for clarity.

- This is the sort of English I will not put up with.

When writing, an author must choose which words give the most clarity and function—even if it includes ending a sentence with a preposition.

CONJUNCTIONS

A conjunction joins two or more words, phrases, or clauses together.

Coordinating conjunctions connect words, phrases, or clauses of equal value, which include *and, but, or, nor, for so,* and *yet.*

- Glass, steel, **and** aluminum, which most people use daily, should be recycled.

Correlative conjunctions are used in pairs: *both/and, either/or, neither/nor, whether/or, not/only, not only/but also,* and *so/as.*

- "Whatever you have, you must **either** use **or** lose."

~Henry Ford

Subordinating conjunctions are used to connect an independent clause (can stand alone) and a dependent clause (needs an independent clause to complete its meaning). Common subordinating conjunctions include the following: *after, although, as, because, before, how, if, once, since, than, that, though, till, until, when, where, whether,* and *while.*

- "It is better to remain silent and be thought a fool **than** to open one's mouth and remove all doubt."

~Abraham Lincoln
Sixteenth President of the United States

Subordinating conjunctions are also used to introduce an independent clause.

- "**Though** we travel the world over to find the beautiful, we must carry it with us or we find it not."

~Ralph Waldo Emerson

INTERJECTIONS

An interjection expresses emotion or surprise, which is often followed by an exclamation point. Grammatically, it stands alone.

- Examples include the following: Hello! Stop! Ha! Ouch! Ugh!

ARTICLES

Although some do not consider an article one of the parts of speech, I am including a brief overview since articles are consistently used in writing. An article is used to introduce a noun which limits or clarifies. Indefinite articles are *a* and *an;* the definite article is *the.*

- **The** earth is covered with 80 percent water, but only **a** small amount is available for human consumption: one percent.

For further study in grammar, I recommend the following two books that every writer should keep on hand for reference: *Strunk & White's, The Elements of Style* and *The Gregg Reference Manual*.

Strunk & White's, The Elements of Style was originally written as a compact study aide by William Strunk, Jr., an English professor at Cornell University. The first edition had only forty-three pages in 1935. Strunk died in 1946 and E.B. White (author of *Charlotte's Web*) was asked to edit the guide for a wider audience, which he did. When E.B. White died, *The Elements of Style* was in its third edition. Now, the book is in its fourth edition after E.B. White's stepson moderately updated it. From the original 43 pages to the current 105 pages, this compact book answers common questions on English usage, form, and style. *The Elements of Style* has influenced writers for years, and it is still one of the best of its kind.

I learned about *The Gregg Reference Manual* by William A. Sabin when I was taking a grammar and proofreading class nearly ten years ago. Not only are the basics of usage, style, grammar, punctuation, and formatting covered, but many excellent examples are included to aid in the study. Solutions to problems in writing are also given in this manual. I have not found one to equal it for clarity and reference. This book is a must for every writer and professional in the publishing and business industry. *The Gregg Reference Manual* was first published in 1951 with many updates through the years. Currently, it is in the tenth edition.

The English language is rich in strong and supple words. Take the time to root around and find the ones you want.[5]

~William Zinsser

5 William Zinsser, *On Writing Well*, HarperCollins, New York, 2006, pg. 32.

CHAPTER FIVE

PUNCTUATION
AND USAGE

Punctuation marks guide your readers. Think of them as language traffic signals: Slow Down. Go That Way. Notice This. Detour. Misleading punctuation can interrupt the flow of ideas and distort meaning, but properly used punctuation helps readers grasp your meaning.[6]

~Jan Venolia
Writer, Editor

The writer only has two ways to be understood in writing—words and punctuation. Punctuation should therefore capture words to the best advantage. The ability to use correct punctuation is an essential skill for every writer. Punctuation can slow, pause, stop, question, or add a punch to thoughts. Incorrectly used, punctuation can change the meaning of the sentence. When properly used, punctuation can add power to it and bring clarity to writing. In this chapter, we will review the basic forms of punctuation.

6   Jan Venolia, *Write Right*. Berkeley, Top Speed Press, Toronto, 2001, pg. 45.

APOSTROPHE '

An apostrophe is used to show possession.

- **Abby's** dog is a beagle and Jack Russell mix.

Important: Do not use an apostrophe with possessive pronouns: *its, hers, yours, ours,* and *theirs.*

An apostrophe is used to form a contraction, indicating an omission of letters. A new word is formed from two individual words as with the following examples.

cannot = can't
would not = wouldn't
you are = you're
she is = she's

Contractions are used in casual writing, but are discouraged in formal writing. Contractions are appropriate to use in dialogue, because just like people, characters generally speak with contractions.

COLON :

A colon has several uses: to introduce a list of nouns, to show that something will be explained further, to separate a title and subtitle, to use after the salutation in a formal or business letter, and to show when information is quoted by a specific person.

1. When a colon is used to introduce a list of nouns, the first letter is generally not capitalized except when proper nouns are used. Note the following examples.

   - Those who are concerned for the environment recycle the following: aluminum, glass, and paper.
   - The following people are going to the party: Ada, Moses, and Bo.

2. A colon is used to explain what follows it and should be used after an independent clause (complete idea). The first word of a phrase is *not capitalized* after a colon when it is not a complete idea.

- Three good reasons for composting are the following: reducing, reusing, and recycling solid wastes.

If the sentence is a complete idea (having a subject and verb) after the colon, the first letter is *capitalized*.

- The answer to reducing trash in landfills is clear: We must recycle.

3. A colon should be used to separate a title and subtitle.
   - Recycling: For the Health of Our Environment

4. In a formal letter or business letter, a colon is used after the salutation. In an informal letter, a comma is used instead of a colon.
   - Formal letter: Dear Sir:
   - Informal letter: Hi Mary,

5. Use a colon when information is quoted by a specific person.
   - Charles Shultz once said: "All you need is love. But a little chocolate now and then doesn't hurt."
   - J.R.R. Tolkien wrote: "Remember what Bilbo used to say: 'It's a dangerous business, Frodo, going out your door. You step onto the road, and if you don't keep your feet, there's no knowing where you might be swept off to.'"[7]

6. When writing time, use a colon between the hour and minutes.
   - 12:30

7. In a bibliographic entry, separate the publication city and publisher.
   - Dorsett, Lyle W. and Mead, Marjorie Lamp, *C.S. Lewis, Letters to Children.* Touchstone, New York: 1985.

8. When citing a biblical passage, use a colon to separate the chapter and verse.
   - Genesis 1:1

---

7   J.R.R. Tolkien, *The Fellowship of the Ring,* Ballantine Books, New York, pg. 82.

COMMA ,

Anyone who can improve a sentence of mine by the omission or placement of a comma is looked upon as my dearest friend.
~George Moore
Irish novelist

The biggest problem with the comma is overuse. Using a comma to show a pause in a sentence is no reason to use one. Rules for commas help with the decision of using one or more. Use common sense as well—if the sentence needs a comma for better understanding, then use one. However, it is best to err on the side of fewer than more with commas. They can be distracting and even annoying to the reader when too many are used.

1. In a series of nouns, terms, or phrases, a comma should be inserted directly after each noun and before the conjunction. Note the following examples:

    • Please bring apples, oranges, or peaches.
    • She washed, dried, and ate the apple.

I heard the following true story while I was taking a grammar class. After hearing the story, it helped me to remember the above rule. Hopefully, it will help you to remember it as well.

A legal case arose against a company who made pencils. They received an order from a customer for 10,000 pencils for each of the following: red, white and blue pencils. The pencil company made 10,000 red pencils and 10,000 white and blue pencils, which was not what the customer wanted. The customer wanted 10,000 red pencils, 10,000 white pencils, and 10,000 blue pencils. The customer asked the pencil company to remake their order. They refused because they filled the order as specified. The customer sued the company and lost the case in court. The court said the pencil company had made the pencils according to the customer's specifications. Because of a misplaced comma, the customer lost the case. The order should have read: 10,000 pencils of each color as follows: Red, white, and blue.

2. Clauses: Commas are used prior to a conjunction (*for, and, or, but, nor, yet, so*) when introducing an independent clause (complete thought).

   • He climbed to the peak of the mountain, and he was thrilled.

3. Do not insert a comma when the clause after the conjunction is not an independent clause.

   • He climbed to the peak of the mountain and was thrilled.

4. A comma should be used to set off introductory elements.

   • *In the morning,* we are leaving for Blue Canyon, California, the city that receives the most snow per year in the United States.

5. Commas are used to separate two or more adjectives before a noun.

   • Zoe longed to be at home in her cozy, stone cottage.

6. A comma is used after an introductory word such as *however, therefore, nevertheless, consequently,* and so on.

   • *However,* the blue whale's whistle is the loudest noise made by an animal.

7. Enclose a parenthetic expression (words that are not necessary to the sentence) between commas.

   • The easiest way to hike the trail, if you have not hiked it before, is to follow the map.

8. If a city's state or country is used after the name of a city, the state or country is considered a parenthetic expression and will need a comma before and after it.

   • In Williamsburg, Virginia, five hundred colonial buildings have been successfully restored.

9. The previous comma rule no longer applies if the state or country is used in a possessive form.

   • Charleston, South Carolina's climate is mild.

10. When a person is addressed in a sentence, the person's name is always considered a parenthetical expression and must have a comma before and after it.

    • I told you, Jen, do not throw that can in the trash when it could be recycled.

11. Do not use a comma when the word *that* is used before a quote.

    • Benjamin Franklin said that "to succeed, jump as quickly at opportunities as you do the conclusions."

12. When the date, month, and year are included, place a comma after the year.

    • July 20, 1969, was when Neil Armstrong first walked on the moon.

13. When no day of the month is used with the month and year, do not use a comma.

    • July 1969 was when Neil Armstrong first walked on the moon.

14. When using historic, international, or military format, no commas are used.

    • Neil Armstrong first walked on the moon 20 July 1969.

EXCLAMATION POINT !

Cut out all those exclamation marks. An exclamation mark is like laughing at your own joke.

~F. Scott Fitzgerald
American Writer

Merriam Webster's definition of "exclamation" is "a sharp or sudden utterance; vehement expression of protest or complaint." An exclamation point should only be used to exclaim as the dictionary definition denotes.

Exclamation points can become ineffective if used too freely. Reserve them for extreme surprise or excitement. For added expression, use words rather than exclamation points—they will exclaim far more. Check for exclamation points in the editing stage, and delete all of them that you can. Never use exclamation points in formal writing.

- Save the exclamation point for a true exclamation: Stop!

If an exclamation point is part of a quote, it should be placed before the quotation marks.

- "Hey! 'Look at that falling star!'"

ELLIPSIS . . .

An ellipsis shows where part of the text has been removed intentionally. If it is in the middle of the text, use three dots with a space before and after the dots.

- "If your actions inspire others to dream more, learn more . . . and become more, you are a leader."

> ~John Quincy Adams
> Sixth President of the United States

If part of the text has been removed at the end of a sentence, place three dots with no space between them, and add the ending punctuation.

- Ralph Waldo Emerson said, "Finish each day and be done with it. You have done what you could. Some blunders and absurdities no doubt crept in; forget them as soon as you can. Tomorrow is a new day; begin it well and serenely…."

When a Scripture is cited and the last part is not used, add three dots with no spaces between them and a period after the quote.

- **"The Lord is my Shepherd…"** (see **Psalm 23:1**).

To indicate a pause in the flow of quoted speech or dialogue, an ellipsis mark should be used.

- "I wonder . . . is it really true?"

HYPHEN, EN DASH, AND EM DASH

Though the differences in the hyphen, em dash, and en dash are small, they each have a purpose, which will be discussed in this section. When using a hyphen, em dash, or en dash, do not use a space before or after them.

Hyphen –

A hyphen is used to connect words or syllables or to divide words into parts. Some words have changed over the years and are now hyphenated because they were frequently used combinations. However, the trend is not to hyphenate words. When in doubt if a word is hyphenated, consult a dictionary. If you cannot find it in the dictionary, it should not be hyphenated.

1. Hyphens are used to combine two or more words to make a compound adjective. The hyphenated word makes one idea.

   - well-known singer, first-class seat, low-budget housing.

2. Adverbs ending with -ly are not hyphenated.

   - carefully conditioned, fully planned

3. Prefixes (all-, self-, ex-) are hyphenated before nouns.

   - all-inclusive project, self-absorbed, ex-manager.

4. Hyphenate compound numbers from twenty-one through ninety-nine.

5. Hyphenate to separate phone numbers and social security numbers.

   - 801-902-7549 (phone number)
   - 381-42-7650 (social security number)

6. Hyphenate all fractions.
   - two-thirds, one-half

7. Hyphenate for clarification as with the following example:
   - re-creation and recreation (the hyphen changes the meaning of the word).

8. Verb and preposition combinations are not (typically) hyphenated.
   - call back, send out, phone in.

En dash —

The en dash is used to mean "through." Use with inclusive dates or numbers. It is longer than the hyphen but shorter than the em dash. The en dash is the width of the letter N on a computer and is longer than a hyphen. It is made by putting a space before and after a hyphen. The computer will then lengthen the hyphen to an en dash. An en dash is also found from the menu of symbols on a computer. Last, an en dash may be typed on some programs by holding down the ALT key while typing 0150 on the numerical pad on the right side of the computer keyboard (ALT + 0150). Do not put a space before or after an en dash.

   - We will be on vacation from July 22–July 29.

Em dash ——

The em dash is the width of the letter M and is longer than a hyphen and en dash. It is used for a strong break in the sentence or for emphasis—to set a word or phrase apart. An em dash can be used like parentheses—to enclose a word or words in a clause—or, it can be used to detach a thought from the sentence. An em dash can be useful in long sentences to give a break in the thought. A space should not be placed between an em dash and the surrounding words.

Some computers do not have the keys to make an em dash, but with most computer programs it can be made by typing two hyphens between two words with no spaces added. The computer will then change it to an em dash. An em dash can also be made from the menu of symbols on a computer. Last, an em dash can be made by holding down the ALT key while typing 0151 on the numerical pad on the right side of the computer keyboard (ALT + 0151). Use the em dash sparingly—and only for effect.

- "There is no shortcut to achievement. Life requires thorough preparation—veneer isn't worth anything."

> ~George Washington Carver
> Scientist, educator

PARENTHESES ( ) AND BRACKETS [ ]

A parenthesis is similar to a dash but adds more personal clarity to a statement. Nonessential information is enclosed inside the parenthesis.

- Abby's class (eighth grade) picked up ten bags of cans to recycle.

Brackets are used to include information inside a direct quote (that was not in the original quote).

- Sam said, "The eighth grade class [fifteen students] won the contest for picking up the most cans."

PERIOD .

Periods are used to stop a complete thought in a sentence. There is not much more to say about the period other than writers do not use it enough. If you find yourself caught in a long sentence, break it up into two sentences.

- "In a moment of decision the best thing you can do is the right thing. The worst you can do is nothing."

> ~Theodore Roosevelt

Periods are also used in initials. Do not put a space between initials, but do add one space after the last initial.

- R.T. Kendall
- U.S.A.

QUESTION MARK ?

A question mark is used at the end of a sentence that is asking a question.

- Did you know that the hottest temperature recorded in the United States was 134 degrees in Death Valley, California?

A question mark is placed inside of the quotation marks when it is part of a quote.

- "Perhaps the very best question that you can memorize and repeat, over and over, is: 'What is the most valuable use of my time right now?'"

~Brian Tracy
Motivational coach

A question mark is placed outside of the quotation mark if the sentence is asking about a quotation (the quotation is not a question).

- Was it Leonardo da Vinci who said: "There are three classes of people: Those who see. Those who see when they are shown. Those who do not see"?

QUOTATION MARKS " "

Double quotation marks are used to enclose direct quotations.

- Charles Schulz said: "Don't worry about the world coming to an end today. It's already tomorrow in Australia."

Double quotations are always after a period, comma, or semi-colon and before a colon (." ," ;" ":). Every double opening quote has a double closing quote ("quote").

Titles of articles from magazines or journals, chapter titles, and television programs are in quotation marks.

Single quotation marks denote a quotation within a quotation.

- Mary explained, "When I spoke to Deb last week, she said, 'I will take care of the problem the first week of May.'"

Every single opening quote has a single closing quote ('single quote').

SEMI-COLON ;

Use the semicolon sparingly in writing. There is typically a better way to write the sentence. A semicolon is used between two independent clauses, and usually it is better to write two separate sentences. However, the following is the correct usage.

- The California condor and the Ivory-billed woodpecker top the list of endangered birds in North America; this was reported by the National Audubon Society in 2006.

When using a coordinating conjunction (and, but, or, nor), do not use a semicolon. Use a comma instead.

- The most endangered mammal in the United States is the black-footed ferret, but they are now beginning a slow recovery in Wyoming.

ITALICS

Italics are used to show emphasis in writing. Be careful with the overuse of italics because they will lose their power.

If quotation marks are not used and a quotation is set apart from the text, italics may be used to show that it is being quoted.

You can't wait for inspiration. You have to go after it with a club.

~Jack London, American writer

Use italics when you use or discuss a particular word in a sentence.

- The word *fragrant* is one of my favorite words.

Words That Are Italicized:

References to:

- newspapers
- pamphlets
- books
- theses and dissertations
- journals and periodicals
- epic poems (with short poems, use quotation marks)
- movies
- full-length operas
- musicals
- plays
- albums (for individual songs, use quotation marks)
- paintings
- drawings
- sculptures
- foreign words
- scientific words for plants and animals
- Note: Chapter titles from magazines, journals, and books are set in quotation marks.

SPACING AFTER PUNCTUATION

Only one space, not two, is placed after punctuation. The one-space rule is an accepted practice in business and publications. With only one space after punctuation, the text looks tighter.

NUMBERS

Spell out all numbers from 1 through 100 and all numbers above 100 that require no more than two words (such as *forty-five million* or *twenty-two thousand*). Numbers in the millions or higher that cannot be expressed in two words should be expressed as follows:

- 14 1/2 million or 14.5 million (in place of 14,500,000)
- 2.4 billion (in place of 2,400,000,000)

TIME

Numbers should be used with a.m. and p.m. (lower case in informal writing).

- 8:45 a.m. and 3:00 p.m.
- a.m.—ante meridian (before noon)
- p.m.—post meridian (post noon)

Do not use a.m. and p.m. with o'clock. O'clock is used in formal writing.

- 1 o'clock or 1:00 p.m.

Do not use a.m. or p.m. with the following: in the morning, in the afternoon, or in the evening. It is redundant to use both.

In books and journals, a.m. and p.m. typically are used with small capitals.

- A.M. and P.M.
- Spell out the numbers of hours, minutes, or seconds.
- Twenty-four hours, not 24 hours.

PERCENTAGES

When writing percentages (%) in formal writing, they should be expressed in figures and the word "percent" spelled out.

- *Not:* 97%. *Instead:* 97 percent.

Punctuation gives the silent page some of the breath of life.
~Sheridan Baker
Author, professor

Chapter Six

Words Commonly Misused and Misspelled

You keep using that word. I do not think it means what you think it means.

> ~ Quote from the movie, *The Princess Bride*

Correct spelling and meaning of a word are crucial for understanding what has been written. Through the progression of language, some words are used in ways that are entirely different from the meaning. Though many people may misuse words in the same way, it does not mean they are correct. Some words are closely related but have a difference that makes one word better to use than another. Since a writer is a wordsmith, it is important to use words correctly. Take the time to write the word you mean to say.

C.S. Lewis put it this way: "The way for a person to develop a style is (a) to know exactly what he wants to say, and (b) to be sure he is saying exactly that. The reader, we must remember, does not start by knowing what we mean. If our words are ambiguous, our meaning will escape him. I sometimes think that writing is like driving sheep down a road. If there is any gate open to the left or the right, the readers will most certainly go into it."[8]

---

8 Wayne Martindale and Jerry Root, *The Quotable Lewis,* Tyndale House Publishers, Wheaton, 1990, pg. 624.

An author can spend hours, weeks, months, even years on a writing project, but when words are misused, and readers do not understand what is written, the credibility of the author declines. Do not depend on a computer grammar/spell-check to catch every mistake because many are not identified. Although the spelling may be correct, the usage may be wrong.

The following is a list of commonly misused and misspelled words with the correct definitions and examples of the correct use.

adverse, averse

- **adverse**—harmful, hostile
  The high cost of chocolate will have an **adverse** effect on sales.

- **averse**—opposed to
  I am **averse** to the smell of smoke.

affect, effect

- **affect**—to influence, to change (most common as a verb)
  The storm will not **affect** the game.

- **effect**—the end result (most common as a noun)
  The **effect** of the storm caused great damage to the stadium.

- **effect**—to bring about (less common as a verb)
  It is imperative that we **effect** the rescue at once.

alright or all right?

Most editors agree that *alright* is NOT all right. "Alright" is acceptable to use in casual writing or as slang, but not in formal writing. When in doubt, use "all right."

- **all right**—all correct
  Are my answers **all right**?

- **all right**—okay, satisfactory
  Are you **all right**?

all together, altogether

- **all together**—everything or everyone
  The Smith family went **all together** to see the Biltmore House in Asheville, North Carolina, the largest house in the United States.

- **altogether**—completely
  The snow stopped **altogether** this afternoon.

allude, refer, elude

- **allude**—to mention indirectly
  He **alluded** to the computer problem, but he did not explain it.

- **refer**—to mention specifically
  Refer to page seven to find the answer.

- **elude**—mentally or physically escape
  Bonnie will **elude** the trap once again.

allusion, delusion, illusion

- **allusion**—indirect reference especially in literature
  In her newest book, there was an **allusion** to Jane Austen's character, Emma.

- **delusion**—mistaken *impression* or wrong idea
  He was under the **delusion** that Mary was in love with him.

- **illusion**—(noun)—false *perception* of reality, belief, or concept
  The **illusion** was that the cat could talk.

among, between

- **among**—use with more than two objects and people
  Among the group, half of them attended the University of North Carolina, the oldest state university in the United States.

- **between**—use with two objects or people
  Between Tom and Mary, they found seven sand dollars.

anxious, eager—be careful not to confuse these terms

- **anxious**—adjective; uneasy, worried, nervous
  The **anxious** student waited for the results of her test.

- **eager**—displaying keen interest or intense desire or impatient expectancy
  Abby was **eager** to help her mom bake cookies.

avoid, evade, or **elude**

These three words are similar because they involve keeping away, but the use of the words is still different.

- **avoid**—keep away from someone or something (neutral tone)
  Patty will **avoid** walking on the newly planted grass.

- **evade**—to escape in a deceptive way (ulterior motive)
  Henry will **evade** paying taxes because he did not report the sale of his property.

- **elude**—to escape or avoid cleverly
  Bob will **elude** his pursuers by hiding in the haystack.

as—do not use as in place of **that, whether,** or **because:**

Incorrect: Tom bought a new guitar **as** it was dented.

Correct: Tom bought a new guitar **because** it was dented.

because and **since** are used with reason clauses

- Florida receives one hundred times more UV rays than Maine **because** it is closer to the equator.
- **Since** ZAO water is the purest water on the market, please bring it to the party.

bring, take

- **bring**—refers to motion toward the speaker
  Bring blueberries, the most nutritious fruit.

- **take**—refers to motion away from the speaker
  Take my book with you, but please bring it back to me Monday.

can, may (could, might)

- **may-might**—indicates permission or possibility
  May I use your computer?

  That container **might** hold enough water.

- **can-could**—indicates ability
  Can Ben really jump six feet high?

  Meredith **could** make barbeque chicken for dinner.

capital, capitol

- **capital**—refers to a city
  The **capital** of Virginia is Richmond.

- **capitol**—a building where the legislature meets
  Abby visited the U.S. **capitol** in Washington, D.C.

climactic, climatic

- **climactic**—from the word *climax* the point of greatest intensity of an event or series
  The two-day **climactic** Battle of Shiloh ended with the Union winning.

- **climatic**—from the word *climate,* meaning meteorological conditions
  The **climatic** conditions are affecting many animals in the South Pole.

come, go

- **come**—drawing near (toward) a location
  Come closer and see the fawn.

- **go**—moving away from a location
  Go to the organic food market and buy broccoli, the most nutritious vegetable.

compliment, complement

- **compliment**—flattering or admiring remark
  I would like to **compliment** you on this delicious cheese soufflé.

- **complement**—something that goes well and completes
  The whipped cream **complements** the strawberries.

continual, continuous (continually, continuously)

- **continual**—frequently repeated but not unceasing
  The **continual** ring of the phone will not stop until someone answers it.

- **continuous**—it never stops
  The earth makes a **continuous** orbit around the sun.

counsel, council

- **counsel**—(noun)—referring to a lawyer who provides legal consultation
  His **counsel** advised the man to speak the truth on the witness stand.

- **counsel**—(verb)—to give advice
  She **counseled** the girl to talk to her parents.

- **council**—assembly or legislators
  The **council** voted to fine those who do not recycle paper and aluminum.

different from or different than?

- **Different than** is a contrasting phrase, not a comparative word. Use **different from** to compare.
  White chocolate is **different from** dark and milk chocolate because it does not contain any chocolate—only cocoa butter, sugar, milk, and flavorings.

elicit, illicit

- **elicit**—verb—meaning to arrive at, to bring forth, to deduce meaning
  His question **elicited** my response.

- **illicit**—adjective—meaning unlawful
  He went to jail because of his **illicit** behavior.

everyday, every day

- **everyday**—used as one word means ordinary
  Rachel's **everyday** routine was to walk to school.

- **every day**—used as two words means daily
  Every day Elisabeth made homemade croissants for the bakery.

i.e.-e.g.—these terms are not interchangeable

- **i.e.**—an abbreviation for the Latin phrase *id est,* which translates to "that is;" i.e. to restate something said in a different way.
  Water dripping from a faucet wastes about eighteen hundred liters of water a month, **i.e.,** the equivalent of twelve bathtubs full of water.

- **e.g.**—an abbreviation for the Latin phrase *exempli gratia,* which translates "for the sake of example" (examples or lists)
  Bring the ingredients for cookies to class; **e.g.,** flour, sugar, butter, and eggs.

except, accept

- **except**—something left out, exclusion
  Deer inhabit all continents **except** Australia and Antarctica.

- **accept**—to receive, entering into an agreement, to join a group
  "If you **accept** the expectations of others, especially negative ones, then you will never change the outcome."
  ~Michael Jordan
  Considered the best basketball player ever

edition, addition

- **edition**—a printed published book, identical copies of a publication offered to the public
  The new **edition** of the book will be printed in October.

- **addition**—adding a component to improve something
  The **addition** of the room adds light to the house.

- The summation of numbers: $5 + 5 = 10$; adding of one thing to another.

emigrate, immigrate

- **emigrate**—to *leave* one country, region, or area and go to another to live permanently
  Many **emigrated** from Russia to the United States in the early 1900s.

- **immigrate**—verb—to *enter* another country and live there
  To find work, many Mexicans **immigrate** to the United States.

entitled, titled—these two words are often misused.

- **entitled**—you have the right to something
  She is **entitled** to the property because her father left the land to her in his will.

- **titled**—the name of a book, article, song, etc.
  The book is **titled** *The Final Quest.*

enquire, inquire—both spellings mean "to ask." However, the common U.S. English spelling is **inquire,** while the British English spelling is **enquire.**

Did you **inquire** about Taylor's new book?

ensure, assure, insure—all three words are used to make a person or thing "sure."

- **ensure**—to make certain; imply a guarantee
  We must **ensure** that all food served is organic.

- **assure**—convince or remove doubt or suspense
  You can be **assured** that I will not tell Mary about the surprise party.
- **insure**—to protect against loss
  Ted's new house is **insured** by Farmer's Insurance Company.

good, well

- **good, better, best**—adjectives used as degrees of difference, but not in health
  Meredith had the **best** creative furniture design in her class.
- **well**—noun—hole in the ground made to draw up water
  The depth of the **well** was one hundred feet.
- **well**—verb—bring to surface
  Tears of joy **welled** up in Perry's eyes when he found his dog.
- **well**—adverb—state of health; incorrect to use "good" in response to state of health
  Shannon felt **well** when she awoke the next morning.

farther, further

- **farther**—refers to literal distance
  Asheville is **farther** from my house than Boone.
- **further**—refers to a greater extent or figurative distance
  Laurel would like to **further** her education.

fewer, less

- **fewer**—used with plural nouns and with numbers or items that can be counted
  Fewer people registered to vote than last year.
- **less**—used with nouns; things that cannot be counted
  Less exertion was needed to finish yesterday's project.

first, firstly

Though some still use firstly, secondly, and thirdly, the recommended usage is first, second, third. Why add -ly to first when it makes the word a syllable longer and, frankly, sounds odd. Stick to **first, second, third**, and **last**—more clear and concise.

forward, foreword

- **forward**—temperament, behavior
  He was too **forward** with Betsy.

- **forward**—toward a position ahead
  Move **forward** in the line.

- **forward**—position on a sports team
  The **forward** on North Carolina State's basketball team is amazing.

- **forward**—send post, email
  Forward my mail to the new address.

- **foreword**—an introductory piece at the beginning of a book; often it is written by someone other than the author. Many misspell foreword by using the word forward.
  The **foreword** in the book was written by Theodore Roosevelt.

imply, infer

- **imply**—to indirectly express or suggest
  Sally **implied** that she was at the restaurant last night.

- **infer**—to assume or conclude from circumstances, evidence, or reasoning

  "It is common error to **infer** that things which are consecutive in order of time have necessarily the relation of cause and effect."

  ~Jacob Bigelow
  Botanist, medical doctor

its, it's

- **its**—possessive pronoun
  The real estate firm was showing all of **its** houses on Sunday.

- **it's**—contraction for it is
  It's going to be a hot day.

irritate, aggravate

- **irritate**—verb; to annoy
  Monty was **irritated** because his sister kept using his cell phone without asking.

- **aggravate**—verb; to make worse
  When he bumped his head again in the same spot, it **aggravated** the existing bruise.

lay, lie—both are verbs and are frequently misused in speech and writing. Because of this, it may be difficult to distinguish the correct usage. To understand which to use, you must understand the meaning of each.

- **lay**—principal parts: lay, laid, laid—(to put or to place); must have an object to complete its meaning.
  1. Please **lay** the keys on the counter (present tense).
  2. Earlier this afternoon, Cassie **laid** the keys on the counter (past tense).
  3. I thought Bess had **laid** the keys on the counter (past participle).

- **lie**—principal parts: lie, lay, lain—(to rest, stay, or recline); refers to a person or thing). The verb does not need an object.
  1. Sonya decided to **lie** in the sun (present tense).
  2. Yesterday, Sonya **lay** in the sun (past tense).
  3. Sonya remembered that she had **lain** in the sun every day (past participle).

lightening, lightning

- **lightening**—to make brighter, illuminate
  The **lightening** of Cara's hair made her look younger.

- **lightning**—an abrupt visible flash of natural charge in the atmosphere
  Every year on the earth, more than 1.4 billion **lightning** flashes occur.

lose, loose

- **lose**—always a verb; to fail at or cannot find
  Every day she **loses** her keys.

- **loose**—(adjective)—not tight
  Claude's **loose** jeans do not fit correctly.

- **loose**—(adjective)—not packaged
  The **loose** tea should be placed in a container.

- **loose**—(verb)—set free
  The captive wolf was **loosed** once his foot healed.

- **loose**—(verb)—untie
  Loosen the tight collar on the puppy.

moot, mute—*moot* point, not mute point. Moot and mute are spelled differently, pronounced differently, and have different meanings.

- **moot**—(adjective)—not open to debate or discussion, doubtful point; pronounced like the sound a cow makes with a "t".
  Since it is a **moot** point, we should not discuss it any longer.

- **moot**—(noun)—in early England, an assembly of people who exercised political powers; an argument or discussion

- **mute**—a person who cannot speak
  Sadly, the child is **mute.**

more than, over—interchangeable when used before numbers, but "more than" is a better choice in formal writing. Exception: When writing about age, "more than" is not suitable.

More than four hundred hotel rooms exist at Heritage International Ministries.

Did you spend **over** $100 at the bookstore?

You must be **over** fifty-five to receive the discount.

of, have—be careful not to use of (preposition) for have (verb). Correct forms are as follows: *could have, might have, ought to have, should have,* and *would have.*

Incorrect: Mary could **of** made the varsity basketball team.

Correct: Mary could **have** made the varsity basketball team.

peak, pique

- **peak**—(noun)—highest point in development, top of a mountain
  The highest mountain **peak** in the world is Mt. Everest.

- **pique**—an emotion of anger, especially from wounded vanity; curiosity; also a type of fabric
  Miranda's attraction was **piqued** when she saw his deep, brown eyes.

principle, principal

- **principle**—can only be used as a noun; a standard law, reason, or rule
  The **principle** rule is to be kind.

- **principal**—noun—highest ranked person or main contributor
  The **principal** of the school was strict.

- **principal**—noun—sum of invested money
  The money Sonya invested had an outstanding return on her **principal.**

- **principal**—adjective—most important
  My **principal** reason for swimming is because I love it.

set, sit

- **set**—transitive verb; to put or to place
  Please **set** the table. You cannot *sit* the table.

- Additional usages: The sun **set**. Let the dough **set**.
- **sit**—principle parts: sit, sat, sat; to be seated
  I will **sit** until he returns.

shown, shone

- **shown**—past participle of show, which means to present for view, to reveal, to make clear, to appear
  Abby had **shown** her art in last Tuesday's exhibition.
- **shone**—past tense and past participle of shine, which means to emit light
  The sun **shone** in the east horizon.

stationary, stationery

- **stationary**—to remain still
  Please remain **stationary** while riding an escalator.
- **stationery**—noun—writing material
  Zoe wrote to her friend on her new **stationery**.

than, then

- **than**—conjunction of comparison
  The Nile River, the longest river in the world, is longer **than** the Amazon River.
- **then**—adverb; indicates time
  Ben graduated from high school and **then** went to the beach.

there, their, they're

- **there**—at a place, point, or matter
  I will meet you **there** tomorrow.
- **their**—belonging to more than two people, places, or things
  Their home is located in the smallest city in the United States, Maza, North Dakota.
- **they're**—contraction for they are
  They're going to Ocracoke Island, North Carolina, this summer which is only accessible by airplane or boat.

to, too, two—three little words that look simple, but they are misused a great deal in writing.

- **to**—preposition—destination, position, or direction of something or someone
  I have been **to** St. Augustine, the oldest city in the United States.

- **too**—adverb—meaning also
  We, **too,** are going to Yosemite Falls, California, the highest waterfall in the United States.

- **two**—adjective—number, more than one and less than three
  Two of the top ten cities to play golf are located in South Carolina: Hilton Head and Myrtle Beach.

toward, towards—both are correct, but **toward** is more commonly used in U.S. English and **towards** in British English. The "s" is not needed, so preferably use **toward.**

whose, who's:

- **whose:** progressive form of who
  "Tis the business of little minds to shrink; but he **whose** heart is firm, and **whose** conscience approves his conduct, will pursue his principles unto death."

  ~Thomas Paine
  Writer, inventor

- **Who's:** contraction of who and is
  Who's going to see the pandas at the National Zoo?

you, your, you're

A typical typo is misusing **your** and **you're.** Unless the word is misspelled, these errors will not be picked up by spell-check. Use the search engine on a Word program for **you, your,** and **you're** to check to ensure that each is used correctly. Proofread the document carefully or you could end up with a sentence like the following.

Incorrect: You're house is beautiful, and I can tell that **your** going to sell it fast.

Correct: Your house is beautiful and I can tell that **you're** going to sell it fast.

The difference between the right word and the almost right word is the difference between lightning and a lightning bug.

~Mark Twain

CHAPTER SEVEN

WRITING: WHERE TO BEGIN

Put it before them briefly so they will read it, clearly so they will appreciate it, picturesquely so they will remember it and, above all, accurately so they will be guided by its light.

~Joseph Pulitzer,
Publisher who helped establish the Pulitzer Prize

Writing is like a path being laid down by the author for readers to follow. The path will need to be cleared of weeds and rocks so the reader does not have to stumble while trying to arrive at the destination. If the writing is understood throughout, when the end of the path comes in the book, readers will not want to stop reading, which is the hope of every author.

To begin writing, the genre and theme or plot must be decided. Answer the following questions about the project in a writing journal:

1. What is the purpose?

2. Who will be reading it?

3. How will it benefit them?

Return to those answers often to remind you of your intended purpose for the book.

TIPS FROM A CLASSIC WRITER

C.S. Lewis was once asked in a letter from a young reader named Joan about how to write. The following is part of the answer that he wrote back to her:

1. Always try to use the language so as to make quite clear what you mean and make sure your sentence couldn't mean anything else.

2. Always prefer the plain direct word to the long vague one. Don't implement promises, but keep them.

3. Never use abstract nouns when concrete ones will do. If you mean "more people died," don't say "mortality rose."

4. In writing, don't use adjectives which merely tell us how you want us to feel about the thing you are describing. I mean, instead of telling us a thing was "terrible," describe it so that we'll be terrified. Don't say it was "delightful;" make us say "delightful" when we've read the description. You see, all those words (horrifying, wonderful, hideous, exquisite) are only like saying to your readers, "Please will you do the job for me."

5. Don't use words too big for the subject. Don't say "infinitely" when you mean "very"; otherwise you'll have no word left when you want to talk about something infinite.[9]

C.S. Lewis' straightforward tips on writing are excellent as his writing confirmed. Creativity does not have to sound ingenious; it just is.

---

9 Lyle W. Dorsett and Marjorie Lamp Mead, *C.S. Lewis, Letters to Children.* Touchstone, New York, 1985, pg. 64.

If the writing structure is flawed, then the passion and heart of the writer will fail in its purpose. If structure is done properly, it is invisible, serving only as a carrier that delivers understanding to the reader. Writing must be clear and concise to achieve its purpose.

INFORMAL AND FORMAL WRITING

The deciding factor between formal and informal writing is the genre of writing, which will change the vocabulary and tone. Different needs in writing call for different styles of writing. Informal writing is generally used when writing a letter to a friend or writing dialogue in a novel. However, if the dialogue occurred in Britain one hundred years ago, the speech will most likely be formal. Colloquialism is using informal words or phrases in conversation, which can be used in informal dialogue in novels. Contractions can be used in informal writing. Avoid using clichés (words that have been overused and have lost much of their power or effectiveness over time), i.e., "better late than never;" "like the pot calling the kettle black." Some clichés are used in informal speech, but they should not be overused.

Formal writing is used for academic and scientific writings and for most articles in magazines as well as some non-fiction. When writing a business letter, always use formal writing. Avoid contractions and using the words I, me, and you in formal writing. Writing from the third person point of view (explained on page 139) will help avoid this. Write according to the occasion and time period. Formal writing can be boring with all these rules, so your job as a writer is to take something boring and make it interesting.

Here are some simple examples of informal and formal writing:

- Informal: I'm not gonna go to the zoo.
- Formal: I am not going to the zoo.

- Informal: Do you get what she's saying?
- Formal: Do you understand her point?

Whatever style you choose to use—informal or formal, be consistent and do not blend the two. Choose the style that is appropriate for whom and what you are writing.

RESEARCH

Once the genre and topic have been decided and before the writing begins, take time to thoroughly research the subject so the writing is not interrupted. Credibility as a writer is at stake in all writing. If the information written is not accurate, readers will be the first to know, and they will lose trust in the writer. Consequently, the purpose of writing will be defeated.

Computers are the most efficient research tool available. Search engines such as Google provide a vast amount of material just by typing a few key words in the search box. Material, which may have taken months, or even years, for authors to research and write, is readily available for those who are skilled on the computer. Read and glean all the material applicable and interesting to the subject before writing. Gather more research than you may need so fewer interruptions will occur when writing.

Books are another effective research tool. If you want to build a library for research, hard copies, of course, are your best option. Books can also be purchased as e-books which are less expensive. Libraries also provide an immense amount of information.

Research your research to make certain all information is correct. When the desired research is checked, be sure to bookmark the reference by saving it in a folder on your computer (a hard copy is also helpful). Crosscheck references to be certain they are accurate in the bibliography if quoted. Reword all information that is not directly quoted to avoid plagiarism. Be sure to get permission to use any quoted material.

Use research wisely. When it is time to use the research, write as though the readers are encountering the subject for the first time. However, a fine line exists in what is written and not written. A hard lesson to learn in writing is not to explain every detail because some things are taken for granted. Every fact that is generally known should not be added. Research is necessary, but be careful not to explain too much.

FOOTNOTES

If quoted material is used in a book or article, sources *must* be cited. Footnotes cite the source of information that has been used from other books, articles, and online sources. When selected, most word programs on computers have a feature that automatically inserts a footnote at the end of the quoted sentence and at the bottom of the page where it is used with automatic numbering. Typically, an automatic line will be inserted above the footnote. Footnotes include the author's name, title of resource, publisher's name and city, date of publication, and page number. On page 102, I used a footnote to cite the resource for the writing tips from C.S. Lewis.

ENDNOTES

Endnotes are used for adding additional comments about the text at the bottom of the page. If the reader chooses not to read the endnotes, they will not serve their purpose. The text will then become confusing because the endnote could contain important information that is needed to understand the text. To alleviate any confusion that might arise from lack of information in the text, avoid using endnotes if possible, except for academic writing. For further information on endnotes, consult *The Gregg Reference Manual.*

BIBLIOGRAPHY

A bibliography is placed at the end of an article, report, or book, and it lists all the resources *consulted or used* in the preparation of the material. Bibliography is typed at the top of the page in capital letters. Entries are listed alphabetically by the author's name, title of work, publisher, publisher's city, and date of publication. Refer to the bibliography at the end of this book on pages 261-262.

APPENDIX

An appendix typically consists of information that the author has chosen not to include as part of the text of the book. However, it is supplementary text included in the back pages of the book that is still important. Examples of material used in an appendix includes the following: explanatory text, questions and answers, maps, tables, lists, charts, definition of words or concepts. As an example, refer to the appendix used in this book on pages 253-259.

INDEX

The purpose of an index is for the reader to be able to locate topics listed in the book quickly. Indexes are alphabetically listed in the back of a book with the page number, indicating where the topic can be found. Reference books typically have an index—especially textbooks, medical dictionaries, "how to" books such as cookbooks, or any book where the author wants the reader to quickly find a topic.

TABLE OF CONTENTS

A table of contents organizes and lists the chapters, usually by titles, in the order in which they appear in a book. A table of contents should be short (less than three pages) so it can easily be referenced.

FOREWORD OR NOT?

A foreword is written by someone else who is likely to be an expert on the subject or genre that the author is writing about. Typically, the person is well-known, and he or she will write about what is brilliant about the book. Some readers do not take the time to read forewords because they want to begin reading the actual book. If you want someone to write a foreword in your book, he or she should be well-known. The foreword should be short and to the point. Also, a good place to add an endorsement from someone well-known is on the back cover.

INTRODUCTION OR PREFACE

An introduction and a preface are basically the same thing. The introduction usually explains why the author wrote the book, giving a glimpse into some of the material written and the importance of it. Introductions are not always read because readers want to actually begin reading the book. In my opinion, it is best to write introductory thoughts in the first chapter, especially if they are important to understanding the book.

THE WRITING BEGINS

Writing is easy. All you have to do is cross out the wrong words.

~Mark Twain

The next part of this chapter is devoted to general guidelines for writing. More detailed information is given for specific genres later in this book. When the purpose, genre, audience, and research have been decided and completed, it is time to write.

OUTLINE

An outline is an organizational tool that helps to put thoughts in order and keep them focused so they will flow well. Like a map, an outline has an origination point, places to visit along the way, and the destination point. If the map is not followed, or certain points are not covered or are deviated from, the destination will not be reached, or, worse, it will be lost. The main points should be established first in an outline.

Next, separate subjects, points to be made, or scenes to take place by chapters. Add quotations and research points in the appropriate chapter outline. Some writers like to use index cards so the subjects or scenes and research can be rearranged. Others prefer to type an outline, dividing the subjects or scenes and research into chapters. Decide which way works best for you.

An outline can take more time than some writers want to give it, but in the end, an outline will help produce articles or books that are more professional and of higher quality than those without outlines.

THE HOOK

"Your first sentence must grab the reader and all of the rest of them must keep him."

~Rick Joyner
Best-selling author

Research confirms that writers have an average of about thirty seconds to seize a potential reader's attention to their book. Most prospective readers look at the back cover synopsis to see if it might interest them. If it does, then they will open the book to the first couple of paragraphs to see if it lives up to the back cover summary. That is all the time writers have to motivate readers to their book. Consequently, some type of hook must be written to generate interest at the beginning of the book. The first sentence, which is the hook, is the most important sentence in an article or book, and it should grab the reader's attention immediately.

Most writers know the importance of the first sentence and paragraph, but spend far too much time at the beginning of the writing project trying to get it right. Struggling for perfect writing in the beginning could set the author up for writer's block. My suggestion is to begin writing and go back to that first sentence and paragraph periodically.

The first part of the writing should begin with something memorable, profound, or exciting. Begin with an important subject or scene, rather than building up to it. As previously stated, writing has changed through the years, so the writer must seize the reader's attention immediately. First lines should be so powerful that the reader must keep reading. Read the following sentences and decide which you prefer:

1. A hot dog consists of the edible part of the muscle of cattle, sheep, swine, or goats, the diaphragm, heart, esophagus, and the muscle found in the lips, snout, or ears.

2. I've often wondered what goes into a hot dog—now I know and I wish I didn't.

William Zinsser wrote the second example as the opening line of an article. By far it is the best choice of the two sentences. The second sentence makes us want to read the article; the first one already tells us everything, so why read it?

At the beginning of a book or article, readers need to become oriented and engaged in the writing. The first paragraph should give a taste of what is to come, intriguing readers to want to keep reading. The first paragraph also needs to be like a springboard to the second by using transition sentences to pull the points together. With determination by the writer, every sentence can be written with the same power and intensity of the first sentence.

In non-fiction, every article or book has an introduction, which includes the reason for the writing. Writing a topic sentence at the beginning of the paragraph will help the writer build the subject. The topic sentence organizes the points to be made within a paragraph and should motivate the reader to want to read more. Each sentence should add something new to the topic sentence and at the same time link the sentences together. Use words that will vividly bring the subject to life. Using terms that are familiar to the reader with something fresh and new will help enlighten the point. Words should be a bond between the writer and the reader.

BUILDING PARAGRAPHS AND CHAPTERS

If an outline has been made, which is recommended, it will help the writer stay on track as more paragraphs are written that build upon the subject. If a detour from the plot or subject is taken, readers will be confused. If the author cannot clarify the subject, the reader never will. For help in writing different genres, refer to that specific chapter in this book.

The writing may begin with an interesting hook to hold the reader's attention for a time, but if intriguing writing is not maintained throughout, the article or book will not be finished. To write a book that is a page-turner should be the highest aspiration of every writer. Writers, who endeavor to ignite the creativity that is within them and write from that place, will reach a whole new level of originality in the books they write.

PARAGRAPH SIZE

Writing is visual. The size of the paragraph catches the eye before the brain processes the words. Short to medium length paragraphs, three to five sentences, look inviting, but when a paragraph takes the whole page or most of it, it will discourage many readers. Why?

Unless the book is for study, a long paragraph can be intimidating, and many readers do not want to take the time to read paragraphs that are too long and involved. In reverse, too many short paragraphs (one or two lines) can be distracting. The paragraph needs to be a pleasing size to encourage readers to keep reading.

While shorter paragraphs are more inviting in America, this is not the case in Europe. I discussed this with a friend of mine who publishes books in Europe, and she said Europeans prefer longer paragraphs. Bottom line: Write the size paragraph for the culture where it will be read.

Points within each subject should be strategically placed within paragraphs to build upon the subject. Each paragraph should amplify the paragraph that precedes it. The last sentence of a previous paragraph should be like a launchpad to the first sentence of the next paragraph. Good writing is confident writing, using fresh words and new thoughts as the paragraphs build upon one another.

As a rule, a new paragraph alerts the reader that a change in subject or something new is about to be added or will deepen the subject. Paragraphs separate ideas, but they should be tied to the subject as a whole.

A narrative is different. Dialogue should be short because most people do not speak in great length. The breaks between the paragraphs allow a pause by either new speakers or thoughts. Fiction needs to be as real as life. Sometimes subjects change drastically between characters in dialogue, and at other times, the subject continues to build for some time. Write dialogue in a natural way. Further instruction for fiction is in Chapter Ten, "Especially for Fiction Writers."

DELETE

When you are on a roll in writing, and you are writing a sentence but cannot seem to make it work, a quick fix is the delete button. An hour can be spent on a sentence and it may still not be right. If it is that difficult to write, then it is not necessary for the subject.

CHAPTERS, SIZE, AND TITLE

Chapters help organize thoughts and generally signify a new thought, scene, character change, or subplot in the story. The subject may need closure for another subject to begin. Something new is getting ready to happen. As with paragraphs, the end of a chapter should be like the springboard to the next. A page-turning hook should be written at the end of each chapter to entice the reader to keep reading.

With chapter size, the same rule applies as with paragraph size. The longer the chapter, the harder it will be for many to commit to finishing the book. Shorter chapters are more inviting because readers can stop sooner due to time constraints. If they know just a page or two is left to read, they will finish the chapter instead of stopping in the middle of it. If they have to stop in the middle of a chapter, it can be difficult to follow the story again, causing them to have to go back and begin the chapter or at least a part of the story again, which can lead to frustration.

Most non-fiction books will need chapter titles due to the variety of content in the book. Fiction books do not always have chapter titles, and it is the choice of the author as to whether it will enhance the book to have them or not. If chapter titles are not used, the chapter title is indicated by a number. However, if chapter titles are used, they should draw interest to the chapter content and be a simple three to five word synopsis. Most readers want to know in two seconds what the chapter is about. My suggestion is to make each chapter title a quick and simple summary of the chapter content.

Usually, when people get to the end of a chapter, they close the book and go to sleep. I deliberately write a book so when the reader gets to the end of the chapter, he or she must turn one more page. When people tell me I've kept them up all night, I feel like I've succeeded.

~ Sidney Sheldon
Academy Award-winning screenwriter, best-selling author

HEADINGS

If the subjects need to change in an article or chapter, it is often helpful to use a heading. A heading alerts readers that something new is being added in the chapter. Headings also help writers stay focused on the point or points to be made within them. Another benefit of headings is that they break up the text, adding space on the page so that it does not look like all words.

An example of a heading on this page is **"Headings."** Headings should be no more than five words and preferably less. Use key words from the paragraphs to form them. Headings should be clear and draw attention to the points that are about to be made. A few catchy headings add interest in a chapter, but too many can be distracting. At least two lines of text should follow a heading if it is located at the bottom of the page.

CONCLUSION

Great is the art of beginning, but greater is the art of ending.
~Henry Wadsworth Longfellow
American Poet, educator

After all the subjects and points from the outline have been made, the next step is the conclusion. The conclusion touches on the main concepts/points in the book or article and is basically a short summary of the writing, but with flair that makes it memorable. When it is time to stop, stop. The writing will be stronger and more memorable if the writing stops when it is time. The reader will be the first to know when the book or article should have ended and did not. Think about what thoughts should be left with the reader. The last sentence should be as powerful as the first in the article or book.

BOOK SIZE

From a publisher's perspective, many factors determine book size. Most publishing companies make an economic decision when formulating lengths and sizes of books. The publisher considers the readers, who are familiar with certain-sized books in particular genres, so they will try to satisfy that need as well. If the author is well-known, more money can be spent enhancing the book size, design, and layout because the publisher knows that it will add value to the book, and they will receive a good return on their investment. For paperbacks, specific size requirements are needed so the book will fit in a shelf pocket at a bookstore. An additional aspect in determining size is for the book to fit the size of the shipping carton. Not only will the publisher be able to pack more books in a carton, but because the books fit tightly in a box, less shifting of the books will ensure that they arrive safely at their destinations.

The type of paper will contribute to the thickness of the book. In addition, every font type and size is different and can significantly change the projected page count of the book after layout. Consequently, publishers determine word counts rather than page counts to establish a size per genre. The word count can give a basic estimation of what the page count will be. When a layout artist arranges and designs the text into a pleasing and readable layout for each page, the exact page count of a book is then determined.

Writers should consider numerous factors in determining the length of a book. As stated, with today's lifestyle, many readers do not have the time to read lengthy books. Some readers might be intimidated by long books because of their educational experience. However, some books need to be long, like scientific or history books, due to the material that needs to be covered. Publishers have their own set of rules for different genres and word counts for manuscripts. However, if the book is exciting, inspirational, and dramatic, setting it apart from other submitted manuscripts, the publisher will most likely work with the writer, even if the word count exceeds what is recommended. Word counts are given at the end of each genre chapter in this book for general guidelines.

In summary, an outstanding book is like an outstanding meal. Intrigue the reader with an appetizer. Build the meal with soup, salad, and a main entrée. Then when the reader is full, add a tantalizing dessert as a final sweet taste to remember the meal.

To get the right word in the right place is a rare achievement. To condense the diffused light of a page of thought into the luminous flash of a single sentence, is worthy to rank as a prize composition just by itself . . . Anybody can have ideas—the difficulty is to express them without squandering a quire of paper on an idea that ought to be reduced to one glittering paragraph.

~Mark Twain

CHAPTER EIGHT

CHOOSING A BOOK TITLE

The title to a work of writing is like a house's front porch . . . It should invite you to come on in.

~Angela Giles Klocke
Writer, photographer

Some studies have shown that the title has 90 percent of the magnetic pulling power to a book. An eye-catching title and book cover are the best ways to advertise the book. If people are drawn to the book by the title, it is the first step to them buying and then reading it. Study headlines in magazines and newspapers; the top stories have intriguing headlines. Just by glancing at those headlines, people will buy the magazine or newspaper. That is the same concept used for books—catchy titles draw interest.

Before you begin writing a manuscript, my recommendation is to give your book a temporary working title. Do not waste time trying to think of a captivating title before the writing begins. It will be easier to think of a title when the writing is finished because you will know exactly what the book is about. After the manuscript is finished, let it sit for a few days. Then return to it and look at it in a fresh way.

The title needs to leap off the page, drawing attention. What does it offer readers? Information? Intrigue? Entertainment? Instruction? Inspiration? Solutions? Think about what is important in the manuscript and write down those words. Use a thesaurus to look up additional words and move them around until something rings right. Some titles are chosen by using wit or taking a meaningful short phrase from the book. The title should create interest, but it should not give away the story. A non-fiction title could give a simple solution, but if a title suggests there is a solution, then it needs to give that solution in the book. Readers will lose faith in the writer if a solution is not given and, of course, the book will not be finished.

The author can be so close to the work that it may be difficult for him or her to be a good judge of the title. When others proofread your manuscript, ask them to be thinking about a title while they are reading it. They may just come up with an appealing one.

At times the title will need explanation. A quick method is to use a subtitle, but limit the words. A title will be stronger with fewer words and will be remembered more easily. The same is true for a subtitle. How many titles do you remember that are long?

For my second book, *Pathway to Purpose,* I had already decided on the title before I finished it. As I wrote the book, I realized those three words were the most effective and intriguing words about my book. A month after the book was published, another book was published with the same title. I was not happy about that, but titles cannot be copyrighted. If ten books are published with the same title, they will all come up on a search engine—which can be good or bad, depending upon which one comes up first. All writers want their book titles to be fresh and unique, so the chance of someone choosing your title is remote, but it does happen. When deciding on a title, be sure to search online to see if it has already been used or if there is another title with a similar name.

When a manuscript is submitted for possible publication, it helps to have a captivating title, but even if you think the title is amazing, there is a good possibility the title will be changed by the publishing company to a more gripping title. Authors may have ideas about their book title and book cover, and the publisher may ask an author what he or she is envisioning for them, but in the end the publisher will choose the title and design the book cover because they know what will sell. Remember, they have been in the business of publishing for years and have vast experience in marketing. Also, typically the more well-known the author, the larger his or her name will be in print and the smaller the title of the book will become.

Occasionally, titles are chosen that have absolutely nothing to do with the book, but again, the thought is to draw attention to the book. This type of title is not recommended often because readers typically think the title tells something about the book, and when it does not, they will become dissatisfied.

We live in an age of surplus information. Titles are crucial. A title must appeal to the reader, or they will read no further. Generate interest with your title, but do not give away the punch line. Take time to choose a creative, meaningful, and intriguing title—it will be time well-spent. Bottom line: Publishers and designers have experience with book titles, and authors most likely will have to submit to their expertise with the selection of the title and cover. After all, writing the book and publishing it are the first hurdles; then the book must sell.

A good title should be like a good metaphor. It should intrigue without being too baffling or too obvious.
~Walker Percy, American author

CHAPTER NINE

THE SKILL
OF EDITING

The most valuable of talents is never using two words when one will do.

~Thomas Jefferson
Third President of the United States

After finally finishing a manuscript, it is crucial to take the time to edit the writing properly. Editing is time well-spent and it could mean the difference between a manuscript being accepted or rejected by a publisher. Think about the initial writing as a piece of silver that is dull, maybe even tarnished. With numerous edits it will change into a beautifully polished and usable piece.

Self-editing is the process of evaluating the writing for content, accuracy, redundancy, misspellings, grammar, and, most importantly, effectiveness. Editing is also the time when the writing may be enhanced by adding seasoning. The writing has been completed, and now the enjoyment begins by adding the finishing touches.

Most first drafts can be cut by at least a third. After the first draft has been edited, the writer will find that even more should be cut to make it more concise. Words are more powerful when they are direct and brief. If something must be said again, it should be stated in a different way by adding life—something new or a different angle that makes the same point.

Editing skills are basic and should be learned by all writers. If you have trouble editing your own work, edit other people's manuscripts. You will learn to detect a good sentence and one that is not. As stated, a good place to meet other writers is at a writers' group. Writers who want to improve their skills will ask for their work to be critiqued and edited—a good place to grow not only in editing but in the craft of writing.

STEP ONE—LET THE MANUSCRIPT REST

After finally finishing writing the manuscript, let it rest for a week. Take a breather. Why? After having worked on a writing project for weeks, months, or even years, distance is needed. The material is too familiar, and your eyes will begin to fill in when a word or explanation may be needed. Typos will be overlooked as well as punctuation.

During the time the project is sitting, some bright ideas will probably come to you. Do not work on the project, but write those ideas down in your writing journal so they will not be forgotten. You will be amazed at the fresh ideas and new zeal that will come when there is distance between you and your writing. After a week, add those brilliant ideas and changes. New life will be added to the project.

STEP TWO—PRINT THE MANUSCRIPT

After working on a computer screen the whole length of the project, it is time to look at your work in a different form—in a new light. As an editor and writer, I can testify to this fact. By reading the manuscript in a different format, it is no longer as familiar-looking, and mistakes and inconsistencies will become obvious. By printing the manuscript, you will be able to make notes and changes in the margins. Another form gives another perspective.

STEP THREE—READING THE MANUSCRIPT

> *Omit needless words. Vigorous writing is concise. A sentence should contain no unnecessary words, a paragraph no unnecessary sentences, for the same reason that a drawing should have no unnecessary lines and a machine no unnecessary parts.*
>
> ~William Strunk, Jr.

A clear sentence is no accident. Rarely is a sentence written perfectly the first time. With practice, a writer will form concise sentences more quickly. Words are tools, and like all tools, it takes practice to use them the correct way. Words are a communication tool, so use them with originality and care by writing clear, tight sentences—to the point.

Every word needs to have a function in the sentence. Unnecessary words add redundancy and weaken any powerful words within the sentence. Adjectives and adverbs can be troublesome words if overused. Refer to pages 62-66 for further study on these parts of speech.

Redundancy means using too many words for explanation. Write with as few words as possible to form the most powerful meaning. Some writers like to repeat themselves by pounding the subject into the readers' heads. When a writer begins to repeat himself, the writing becomes boring, and the possibility of the reader not finishing the book or article increases. When redundant words are deleted, the sentence will become stronger because there is no fluff to interrupt the true meaning. However, sometimes thoughts are repeated for retention, which is fine, but again, do not overdo it. Clarity is having the ability to express clearly. While reading your manuscript, look for reduncancy and delete those parts.

When the reader comprehends the words of the writer, a connection occurs. Words become a link to understanding the new ideas, thoughts, and passions of the writer. If, however, the writer seeks to parade his intellectual ability and choose words that are not easily understood, disastrous results will occur. Such was the case with a memo President Franklin D. Roosevelt received, which was written by his own government officials concerning a blackout order from 1942. Try to understand the following paragraph:

Such preparations shall be made as will completely obscure all federal buildings and non-federal buildings occupied by the federal government during an air raid for any period of time from visibility by reason of internal or external illumination.

After reading the memo, the following was President Roosevelt's response: "Tell them that in the buildings where they have to keep the work going to put something across the windows!" I like President Roosevelt's reply; it was clear and to the point. I have never understood why some people (lawyers in particular) write so people cannot understand the meaning—it is almost like what they write is a secret and they want it to stay that way.

Have you ever been reading a book and had to stop and look up a word in a dictionary? Not only can this be aggravating, but if there are several large words in an article or book, it can make the reader feel unintelligent. Words need to be communicated so that others can understand. Why write if the meaning is not clear? Big words, long sentences, and redundancy add up to writing that is not only boring, but unreadable.

As stated, every word should count in a sentence. Let's look at the following phrases used by writers that should be deleted:

- "It's interesting to note."

If it so interesting, why does the writer need to tell us before-hand? Also, once a writer states it is interesting to note, the reader is going to judge the sentence to see if it is interesting.

- "It should be pointed out."
  If the words are strong enough to stand alone, then they should not have to be pointed out. Sometimes the best way to make a point is to tell a story. Stories are well-remembered.

- "The fact is...." Facts are information; why does the reader need to be told a fact is coming before it is written?

- "Needless to say...." It *is* needless to say, if that is written first!

The following is a sampling of redundant phrases. All can be shortened to remove clutter from the sentence. The corrected word follows the phrase.

- close proximity: proximity
- absolutely essential: essential
- past history: history
- end result: result
- already exists: exists
- completely destroyed: destroyed
- summarize briefly: summarize
- free gift: gift
- exactly identical: identical
- arrived at the conclusion: concluded
- first and foremost: first
- personal opinion: opinion
- clearly evident: evident
- follow after: after
- join together: join
- group together: group

- large in size: large
- regular routine: routine
- may possibly: may
- original founder: founder
- unexpected surprise: surprise
- more and more: often
- new breakthrough: breakthrough
- personally responsible: responsible
- repeat again: repeat
- refer back: refer
- current status: current
- tired cliché: cliché
- while at the same time: while

WORDINESS

This report, by its very length, defends itself against the risk of being read.

~Winston Churchill

One of the secrets to good writing is to strip every sentence to its cleanest or clearest components. Every word needs to be examined in a sentence. If a word serves no function, it should be deleted. Writing should be simple enough to understand, yet interesting. The following are wordy sentences that need to be shortened. The edited sentences follow.

- At this point in time, we can't ascertain the reason as to why the screen door was left open (19 words).
  Revised: We don't know why the screen door was left open (10 words).

- The point I wish to make is that fish sleep with their eyes open (14 words).
  Revised: Fish sleep with their eyes open (7 words).

- In the event that the friends of Matthew arrive after 12 midnight, please call each and every friend of his (20 words).
  Revised: If Matthew's friends arrive after midnight, please call all his friends (11 words).

By using fewer words, writing will be concise and clear. It will take extra time to write that way, but the sentence will be far stronger and more precise.

AVOID EXPLETIVES

The word *expletive* comes from the Latin word *explere*, which means "to fill." In writing, expletives are meaningless words used to "fill." A word or phrase that does not add to the meaning of a sentence is an expletive. A word that temporarily takes the place of a subject/object is an expletive. Some examples are the following: There are; there is; it is.

Writers should avoid beginning sentences with expletives. Expletives delay the subject and can water down the writing. Occasionally, writers need to use expletives, but *only* occasionally. The best way to write tight, clear sentences is to look at every word to see if it is beneficial.

- Original: There are more than fifteen thousand types of species which are threatened to become extinct (15 words).
  Revised: More than fifteen thousand types of species are threatened to become extinct (12 words).

- Original: It is hoped that every household will replace ordinary bulbs with CFL bulbs to help conserve energy (17 words).
  Revised: Every household should replace ordinary bulbs with CFL bulbs to conserve energy (12 words).

A poorly constructed sentence is like a half-drawn picture. It can be read too many ways. Clarity is extremely important. If a sentence is not clear, mark it during this stage to be changed.

The following is a sample sentence that needs work. Read the following sentence, and then look at the corrected sentence below it.

- Everyone of the workers have bought less soft drinks in the pass six months then they did the previous six month period.

Corrected sentence:

- **Every one** of the workers **has** bought **fewer** soft drinks in the **past** six months **than** they did **in** the previous **six-month** period.

BE CAREFUL WITH WORDING

If the order of the words is arranged incorrectly in a sentence, confusing and sometimes hilarious results occur.

- I went to a restaurant that serves "breakfast at any time." So I ordered French Toast during the Renaissance.

~Stephen Wright

Novelist

Check out these actual sentences used in advertisements.

- Kids with gas eat free.
- Illiterate? Write for free help.
- Parking for drive-thru only.
- For anyone who has children and doesn't know it, there is a day care center on the first floor.

Although the meaning is somewhere, these sentences are confusing and give little confidence in the advertisement or the writer. Misplaced modifiers are mistakes not easily forgotten.

Writing should have a natural flow in the content. By reading for content you will find where the problems exist. Do not stop and correct every mistake—just mark them on a hard copy and keep reading. The repair stage will come later in the proofreading process. Consider that you are someone else reading the manuscript for the first time. Check for the following while editing:

- Is the first sentence of the book intriguing?
- Is the first sentence and paragraph at the beginning of each chapter gripping?
- Is the last paragraph of each chapter a page turner?
- Look for flow in the writing (mark abrupt changes).
- Is the writing clear and concise?
- Look for long sentences, and make them into two if necessary.
- Check for rhythm (mark paragraphs that need to be moved or are out of place).
- Look for repeated themes. Too much repetition will weaken the power of the writing.
- Check for redundancies.
- Mark odd-sounding words and misused words (if you happen to see them while editing, mark them, but these are most often caught in the proofreading stage).
- Check for awkward sentences throughout.
- Check for missing information.
- Avoid jargon. If you use technical terms, explain in comprehendible language.
- Are there any glitches (distractions that take away from the subject matter in each chapter)?
- Was the purpose accomplished?
- Does every page hold your interest?
- Were all questions answered that were posed in the writing?
- Are loose ends tied?
- Does the conclusion on the last page of the book leave the reader with something memorable?

STEP FOUR—READ IT OUT LOUD

Though reading a manuscript out loud may seem to be a meaningless step, I assure you it is an excellent use of time. By reading out loud, the words will be read slower than when read silently on a computer screen. Errors will pop out when they never did before. Nuances of rhythm and interpretation will be discovered and will need to be changed. While researching for this book, I discovered that some publishing houses will not accept a manuscript unless it has been read out loud by the author. Some said it was the most important tip they could give aspiring writers.

STEP FIVE—EDITING STAGE

During this step, you will make the content changes that have been notated in Steps Three and Four. After the editing changes have been made, it now becomes the second draft. The writing must be read again to make certain the new material that was added or text that was deleted flows with the previous writing. The same steps should be taken as above to ensure that the writing is strengthened. You are now in the stage of refining the book. I cannot stress enough the importance of carefully working on as many drafts as it takes to get the writing in the best shape possible. Repeat this step as many times as it takes to make certain that the writing is flowing well and that the content is strong and, most importantly, has achieved its purpose.

STEP SIX—PROOFREADING STAGE

If the material is becoming too familiar again, put it down for a few days and then return later. Step Six will take much concentration, so you want to be fresh when you begin. If you are satisfied that the content has been edited to the best of your ability, you can now begin the proofreading stage. The reason this is done separately is because it is too difficult to check for editing changes such as content and grammar and spelling errors at the same time. I recommend proofreading a printed manuscript.

- Checking for grammar, punctuation, and spelling are the last areas a writer should proofread. Please refer to Chapter Six, "Words Commonly Misused and Misspelled." Mark any words that are questionable.

- Spell-check on the computer is helpful, but keep in mind, wrong usage of a word is not caught by a computer. For example, shown and shone are spelled correctly, but the definitions are different. Affect and effect are used incorrectly by many, and the computer may not show you the correct usage. Use spell-check on your computer, but remember you will still need to personally check for misused and misspelled words in the manuscript thoroughly. Trivial errors like this can downgrade even the most brilliant writing.

- Tenses should be checked. If your project is written in present tense, stay there.

- Check for passive writing and change to active writing. See pages 51-52 for further guidelines on this type of writing. Remove any weak nouns, verbs, and modifiers.

- Check writing carefully, searching for repeated or overused words. Use synonyms to help replace them.

- Look for any adjective-noun combinations that can be replaced with stronger, more specific nouns.

- *You, you're,* and *your* are commonly misspelled/misused in writing. Use the find feature on your computer to search for every *you.* By typing *you,* the computer will also search for *you're and your.* Also check *than* and *then,* which are also frequently misused or misspelled.

- Check for the seven conjunctions using your find feature: *and, but, for, or, nor, so, yet.* A comma should come before every conjunction when there is an independent clause (clause has a subject and predicate) before the conjunction.

- Prune weak words: really, so, very, a little, sort of, kind of, rather, quite, I think, pretty much, in a sense, it seems, and any other weak words. These words disqualify what you are writing. Refer to Chapter Four on "The Basics of Grammar" for further instruction.

- Check all punctuation to see if it is correctly used. Do not trust the punctuation check on your computer to catch every error.

- Double-check all references, quotes, and sources. Reminder: Get permission if any quotes are used from a book.

Let your writing sit for a few days again after finishing Step Six. Then go back and proofread it again, checking for other errors. You may have made more errors when making changes.

STEP SEVEN—OPINIONS

It is impossible to write one's best if nobody else has a look at the result.[10]

~C.S. Lewis

Ask friends to read your manuscript or article. Unbiased, honest opinions are valuable. Develop a hard skin and receive what is given from others about your work. Being open to change will cause growth in writing skills, and the veins of creativity will go to an even deeper level. Never stop learning and growing as a writer. Learn from others.

---

10 Wayne Martindale and Jerry Root, *The Quotable Lewis,* Tyndale House Publishers, Wheaton, 1990, pg. 623

After all, they will not be as harsh as those reading your manuscript for possible publication. Ask them to note anything in the manuscript that needs clarification. Most important to know is how your work affected them. Decide whether their ideas warrant using or not. You are the editor at this point. Repeat this process with other friends until you are satisfied that the manuscript is concise and clear.

I appreciate it when others read my work and suggest changes. I have not always been that way, but I learned that others who are reading my manuscript with new eyes will see things that I may have missed or thought were clear.

A writer has the full picture or all the pieces to a puzzle, and then he or she gives those pieces to a reader. The reader tries to put all the pieces back together to complete the puzzle. The difficulty comes to the reader when a piece or several pieces are missing. That is the value of others reading your writing. They will be able to point out something that is missing or something they do not understand. If you will take positive criticism at face value, you will grow as a writer. Most of the changes suggested by honest friends are usually excellent and should be incorporated.

An unpublished manuscript needs to be in the best shape possible before being sent to a publisher. The chances rise for publishing the book when the writer takes the time to carefully correct mistakes. The less work editors and proofreaders have to do on your book, the happier the publisher will be with your initial work.

STEP EIGHT—MAKE FINAL CHANGES

The final step in completing the editing process is to read the manuscript one last time after all changes have been made. Read the manuscript in whatever form you are the most likely to find errors (computer screen, out loud, printed). This is the last and final time to make any changes before sending it to a publisher. Take your time. When you are certain that the manuscript is clean, clear, and amazing, and in the best possible shape, it is ready to send to a publisher.

Chapter Fifteen, "Editors, Agents, and Manuscript Formatting," explains what editors and agents do and how to submit a manuscript for possible publication.

There is a difference between a book of two hundred pages from the very beginning, and a book of two hundred pages which is the result of an original eight hundred pages. The six hundred are there. Only you don't see them.

~Elie Wiesel
Writer, professor, political activist

CHAPTER TEN

ESPECIALLY FOR FICTION WRITERS

We want a story that starts out with an earthquake and works its way up to a climax.

~ Samuel Goldwyn
Academy Award and Golden Globe Award-winning producer

The greatest skill of a fiction writer is the ability to tell a story. If the storytelling is not strong, all the flaws in the writing will become blatant. The job of the novelist is to write a story that is convincing and true, never seeming like fiction. The possibilities are as vast as the imagination. This chapter is an accumulation of study and experience to help prepare and guide those who desire to write fiction creatively.

WHERE TO BEGIN

Novelists write stories from ideas that come in various ways. A sudden thought can birth an idea, or maybe an idea will come in a conversation. Perhaps something has happened in your life that sparks a creative plot. As mentioned, the storyline for my fictional book, *The Chosen Path,* came first through a dream. I awoke remembering vivid images of a girl on an amazing journey. Many novelists are inspired by reality, adding spice or variety to make scenes memorable. Ideas can come in the oddest places and moments. Keep a writing journal with you at all times so that you can write down ideas.

C. S. Lewis wrote *The Lion, the Witch, and the Wardrobe* from pictures in his vivid imagination. He explained that "the actual writing began with an image. I see pictures . . . I have no idea whether this is the usual way of writing stories, still less whether it is the best. It is the only one I know: images come first."[11]

When you finally arrive with a brilliant idea for a story, do not talk about it. If you are excited about the plot (and you should be), the more you talk about it, the more your excitement will be lost, which may cause you to never write the book. Also, the plot can change as you tell it, perhaps even diluting it. Tell your friends you are writing a novel, but that they will just have to wait and read the manuscript. (This is a good way to get them to proofread it, too.) Bottom line: Keep your excitement alive by writing it, not telling it. Love and guard the plot.

LEARN FROM MOVIES

Because most movies are action-packed, a writer can learn much from watching a movie. A dilemma always needs to be solved in a movie, so watch to see when the conflict begins and how it is solved. Most screenwriters have the gift of knowing how long a scene or plot should last and when to switch to a new one, which is also an important skill of a fiction writer. That same type of excitement, drama, comedy, and punch lines in movies should also be written in books.

Pay attention to how information is given through different parts in a movie—narration, setting, conflicts, rising action, climax, and

---

11 Lyle W. Dorsett and Marjorie Lamp Mead, *C.S. Lewis, Letters to Children,* Touchstone, New York, 1985, pgs. 5-6.

so on. Movies have the advantage of giving viewers vivid scenes. A fiction writer is given the task of writing words so the reader can imagine the scene. In the best fiction writing, the reader is not being told about the scene but is experiencing it.

In movies, scenes are viewed in panoramic colors. Scenes are the background for emotions such as joy, fear, anger, or sadness which are expressed through action or dialogue between characters. Scenes can draw the viewer deeply into the movie. Likewise, by adding some of the same techniques that movies use with dialogue in scenes, writing can become more exciting. The author needs to create a scene that enables the reader to clearly imagine the character in the setting, reflecting his facial expressions through dialogue and actions. When readers are able to imagine a scene as if they were there, the writer has succeeded.

TARGET AUDIENCE

The storyline will determine the target audience for a novel. Before the writing begins, the age group for which the book is intended needs to be determined. This does not mean that other age groups will not read it, but it will help the writer decide how to write the book. Writing techniques change with different age groups and genres. Choose an appropriate style for the target audience: tone of voice, level of formality, plot, and vocabulary.

WRITER'S VOICE

All writers need their own recognizable and signature voice in writing. Some might call it a writer's "style," but it is more than that. By reading several books from a particular author, the unique voice of the writer will shine through. It cannot be taught and it is not found by copying other writers. The best way to find your voice or style in writing is to write often. Soon, your voice will become recognizable, even cherished, by those who read it.

A writer's voice is not character alone, it is not style alone; it is far more. A writer's voice like the stroke of an artist's brush—is the thumbprint of her whole person—her idea, wit, humor, passions, rhythms.

~Patricia Lee Gauch
Author and editor of children's literature

POINT OF VIEW: FIRST, SECOND, OR THIRD PERSON

Each story is told through a point of view. Depending upon which point of view is chosen, the format and the way the book is written will change, so it should be decided before writing. A measure of one's writing ability is how effective the point of view is used. The point of view is written in three tenses: first person (I, me, my, we, and our), second person (you and your), and third person (he, she, they, their, his, hers, him, her). Writers need to be careful not to go back and forth with different points of view between two characters' emotions in the same scene. Keep it clear.

First Person

First person is becoming more popular to use in novels, and it is the most distinct point of view. Written from the "I" point of view, it is often used in detective novels and thrillers. The reader experiences the novel through the eyes of the protagonist (main character) who interacts with other characters in the story. Information can be withheld due to how the main character views an event. Emotions such as joy and fear are felt intensely by readers in first person. However, limitations occur because the reader can only know what the main character feels and sees. The reader has the task of deciding what really happens.

Second Person

Few novels are written in the second person point of view. Statements are implied from the "you" point of view. It can be difficult to write a novel in second person and tiresome for the reader if the author is not a master of this point of view. However, if well-written, readers will feel like they are in the midst of the action. Some authors blend second with first and third person, but again the author must be in control and know how to accomplish this. Otherwise, it can become perplexing to the reader. Writing in second person is most effective when used in small measure (articles).

Third Person

During the twentieth century, third person became the most popular narrative. Third person is the most versatile of tenses and is recommended for novels (the over-the-shoulder type of perspective). This tense uses such phrases as "she said" and "he thought." Third person is simple and easy to read and is widely accepted by publishers. Most novels are written in third person omniscient or third person limited.

Third Person Omniscient

The narrator reveals what is happening through characters' thoughts. The advantage of third person omniscient is that readers are able to see through the eyes of various characters, understanding and viewing different perspectives that can help move the plot forward. No single character may know all of the thoughts, feelings, even dreams of other characters—the reader has that advantage.

Third Person Limited

The story is told through a character's "limited" perspective. The reader does not know any more information than what one character knows, sees, and feels. Some think the third person limited is the truest point of view because it is projected through only one person.

Third Person Objective

In third person objective, a story is told without any details of a character's thoughts. An objective point of view is given (fly on the wall perspective). Newspaper articles typically use this type of view.

How to Choose a Point of View

Become familiar with authors who have written from first, second, and third points of view. Some work better than others with different story types. Try different points of view for the first few pages of your novel and see which feels the most comfortable for you to write. Books can switch in point of view; no rule states that you have to stay within the same one. However, if you switch the point of view, it must be clear to the reader. Typically, it is best to stay with one.

FLASHBACK

Flashback is used to interrupt the story so the reader can go back in time to review an event or scene. Flashbacks could be used to show an incident or incidents that made a character a certain way—whether it is being shy, angry all the time, unhappy, not trusting, and so on. Perhaps a disaster, natural event, or accident happened that needs to be explained to understand the present. If flashback is used, write it carefully so the reader will understand that it is not happening in the present. Flashbacks should only be used if the information is important to understand in the story because it can be confusing if not written correctly.

CHRONOLOGICAL ORDER

Chronological order is the time sequence in a story. Fictional writers need to decide if a scene should last a day, a week, or even longer. The length should depend on the importance. Some scenes may take a chapter to write, while others may need a page. Decide what is important in the story, and write accordingly.

PLOT

The plot is the sequence of planned events and actions of the characters that give the story meaning. The tempo of the story can be slowed down or made faster, depending on the action taking place. As the story progresses, so should the action.

Typically, the first part of a plot sequence is called the *exposition*. Information the reader needs to know is revealed, but it does not usually move the story forward. The main characters and setting are introduced. A good way to think about exposition is "exposing" the plot. Quick and simple information is given so readers are permitted to deduce their own conclusions, which adds to the intrigue of the story.

The following are five typical parts of a plot:

1. **Conflict:** At the beginning of a story, a conflict or challenge should develop that will need to be solved. This conflict propels the story forward.

2. **Complications:** Events in the plot should occur to increase the conflict—typically two forces meet. These complications could be internal (inside the character) or external (outside the character).

3. **Rising Action:** The drama should increase through a series of events, escalating the tension in the story.

4. **Climax:** The plot's turning point—the revealing moment, the greatest suspense, and one of the most intense parts in the story. The climax leaves the reader wondering what will happen next—how will the suspense be solved?

5. **Resolution:** The drama should begin to subside and the complications from the conflict should be resolved. The last part of the book should eliminate all misunderstandings and secrets.

CHARACTER-DRIVEN AND EVENT-DRIVEN PLOTS

In a character-driven plot, the main character (protagonist) is forced into action. The protagonist must have a need, conflict, or challenge—something must be solved. Usually an antagonist (enemy) of the main character is either causing the conflict or has attributed to it. This conflict could be experienced through an internal conflict—an emotional or internal flaw within the character that needs to be overcome, or an external conflict, a situation that causes conflict. Plot complications occur, entangling the character even deeper into the growing conflict. The plot should twist in the middle of the story and last until the end, when it is then solved, bringing the conclusion to the character's conflict. Action and excitement are mixed in a character-driven plot, but the reader typically remembers characters rather than the action or event. Through all the trials that the main character has suffered and overcome, some visible internal growth should occur in the character. Think of it this way: In the Olympics, we do not know who will win the singles ice skating gold medal until the very end of the competition. We have our favorites and this keeps us watching until the last skater has competed and then we see who wins.

Unusual plots make great stories. The character-driven plot of *The Lord of the Rings* could be stated in one sentence: The evil ring that rules all rings must be destroyed so that Middle Earth can once again live in peace. The strength of Tolkien's storyline is brilliantly woven in the plot through the characters. Setting, conflicts, climax, and the conclusion add depth to the plot. The main character, Frodo (protagonist), has a goal of destroying the ring while Sauron, Saruman, and Gollum (antagonists) are trying to stop him. Frodo also has the internal conflict of a growing attachment to the ring which he knows must be destroyed. Supporting characters help him but ultimately it is Frodo's task to destroy the ring. Defining experiences happen— predictable and unpredictable. Intrigue keeps the readers interested in the story until the end. The crises were not solved too easily or quickly. Victories happened along the way with some defeat, but the main conflict was not resolved until the last part of the book.

An event-driven plot is a less popular form of fiction writing but can still be exciting. The plot advances through external events, which are natural or human-initiated. Examples of event-driven plots include those about war, events on 9/11, an avalanche, snowstorm, tornado, and floods. *The Perfect Storm: A True Story of Men Against the Sea* by Sebastian Junger is an example of an event-driven story. One of the worst storms in history was created by such a rare meteorological combination that it was deemed the "perfect storm." The captain and crew on the Andrea Gail face the tempest in all its fury. It was a storm against man.

In an event-driven story, a character's inner strength and confidence rises to face the challenge set before him. Event-driven stories enthrall readers through the excitement of events. The characters are important to the action, but the action is most remembered. For example, in an event-driven story, a hurricane could devastate a popular island resort and many are injured as a result. The hurricane caused the conflict, but many fought against all odds to save the injured—some were lost, but many were found. Heroes and heroines rise to the occasion because of the events that drove them to act.

In fiction, conflict/struggle is a necessary ingredient. A hook (conflict) at the beginning of the story is important, but other hooks need to be added throughout the story so the reader will remain engrossed in the book. However, too much conflict is overwhelming. A balance of conflict, adventure, and some emotional pull should occur to keep the reader turning pages. As the writer builds the struggle, the emotions of the character should be felt. Readers should feel like they are in the scene, seeing and feeling the same emotions as the characters in the story. Both character-driven and event-driven stories should have a climatic confrontation and then loose ends should be tied up, finalizing the story.

SUBPLOTS

At least one subplot is crucial in fiction. Subplots may connect to main plots, in time, place, or in another significant theme, and they usually involve supporting characters. A subplot takes less writing space than the main plot of the story, but it serves to build and push the main plot forward and adds richness to the story. For example, a subplot could show where the villain may be planning some evil for the main character, like a foreshadowing of an event to come.

In *The Lord of the Rings*, subplots are sewn throughout the book to push the plot forward. While Frodo and Sam (Frodo's companion on their journey) are on a dangerous quest to destroy the ring of power in Mount Doom, the subplots include the characters of Gandalf, Aragorn, Legolas, Gimli, and a host of others who are fighting the evil armies of Sauron and Saruman to give Frodo and Sam the chance to accomplish their purpose.

PLANNING THE PLOT AND SUBPLOT

Begin by listing chapters, and write several sentences about the plot/subplot for each chapter in an outline. Once the chapter ideas are written, you may see that the subplot in Chapter Five would be best in Chapter Two and the plan for Chapter Seven is not necessary.

Each chapter should have a plan to be attention-grabbing with some intense scenes. Maintaining an emotional pull so that the reader wants to finish the book is a key element in writing fiction. Add surprises but not too many. Most certainly plots and subplots will change by the end, but at least a rough outline will help to stay on track.

THE IMPORTANCE OF RESEARCH

Researched material brings authenticity and accuracy to a novel. When I was writing *The Chosen Path,* Feena had to teach Zoe how to become a skilled archer. To be able to write that scene, I needed to understand not only the skill of archery but how to teach someone to become a skilled archer. In high school, I took archery classes and remembered some of the skill but not enough to write about it accurately. I had to do a lot of research for it to seem realistic in my novel.

For study purposes, I will use the example of how to research material for a historical novel. The library is an excellent place to begin the study. Many books are written on historical facts for specific time periods. Also, be sure to check out books written during that time period to ensure accuracy. Internet research will yield a vast amount of information as well. Research the research for accuracy.

Another helpful idea is to visit the town where the novel will be taking place. Museums, historical sites, and historians in the town will be a valuable source of accurate information. Excitement will come as new ideas for the novel formulate from facts discovered in the time period. Setting and narrative will come alive and flow better. To be successful in a historical novel, writing must be logical and consistent for that time. If you are not willing to research the material needed for a historical novel, do not attempt to write one.

The following are some of the basic questions that should be researched:

1. Setting during time period (housing, what the town was like, unique features about the area)
2. Living conditions
3. Home life
4. Dress according to the character's station in life (poor to aristocratic)
5. Language differences among classes
6. Occupations and how they were performed
7. Food—types of traditional food among classes
8. Transportation
9. Music and leisure activities
10. Medicine—level of expertise of doctors

Researching is like doing detective work—uncovering facts until the case is solved. It can be a lot of fun, and besides, you will gain knowledge as a result. Be sure to get permission if any quotes are used from a published book.

THE STORY BEGINS

For learning purposes, I am going to use the character-driven plot as an example for learning more about writing fiction. The introduction of a novel should begin with meeting the main character in a memorable setting and in an exciting scene. Answer the following questions:

1. Where are we?
2. What's the conflict?
3. Who's involved? Readers should know right away which character is the main character.

By answering these questions and then writing the answers, the reader will begin to connect to the story. The reader needs to visualize the main character and setting right away to feel involved in the story to keep reading it. If the author fails to do this, the reader will feel confused and disoriented and will stop reading. As stated, the first paragraph and page must grab the reader's attention immediately.

SETTING

Don't tell me the moon is shining; show me the glint of light on broken glass.

~Anton Chekhov
Russian short story writer and playwright

The setting is the location of the story's action and the time in which it takes place. Every setting needs to further the plot. Do not give away too much too early in the setting. Determine what to write according to the importance of the action that is happening.

Keep the scene real, just like in life. If a character is swimming, she cannot have an intimate conversation with someone on shore. Think about the character's moves in every scene and make them realistic. Scenes should not slow the progress of the novel but add depth and pace.

Settings can be imaginatively used to tell about the characters. Settings usually include the following, but remember it is not necessary to add all of these elements.

1. **Location**: Where is the story taking place? In the Blue Ridge Mountains, the Sahara Desert, Denver, or a creepy forest? The setting should indicate something about to happen: a snowstorm where a main character is injured, the forest where a rattler is about to strike, a person lost at sea, a defining phone call, or meeting in a restaurant, and so on. The setting is a backdrop for conflict.

2. **Time**: What is the historical period or perhaps the time of day, depending on the action in the scene?

3. **Season**: Is it winter, summer, spring, or fall? The setting may indicate the season so it may not be necessary to tell it. If the month of the year is important to the story, add it. The weather might affect the following.

4. **Atmosphere**: Does the weather reflect the character's mood? Is he sunny to reflect happiness or sunny, mocking his sadness? The atmosphere may be cold, but the character's feelings are warm because she has fallen in love. Use the atmosphere to the best advantage in writing.

5. **Living environment:** What type of environment does the character live in? If she is poor, the setting should reflect this. If she is wealthy, her speech and mannerisms should be written to show her affluence. Are there any special customs to show her heritage in her living environment?

In Jane Austen's *Pride and Prejudice*, when Elizabeth Bennet and her aunt and uncle first see Mr. Darcy's home, Pemberley, Elizabeth is enthralled. The description of the setting allows the reader to visualize the greatness of the estate:

They gradually ascended for half a mile, and then found themselves at the top of a considerable eminence, where the wood ceased, and the eye was instantly caught by Pemberley House, situated on the opposite side of a valley, into which the road with some abruptness wound. It was a large, handsome, stone building, standing well on rising ground, and backed by a ridge of high woody hills; and in the front a stream of some natural importance was swelled into greater, but without any artificial appearance. Its banks were neither formal nor falsely adored. Elizabeth was delighted. She had never seen a place for which nature had done more, or where natural beauty had been so little counteracted by an awkward taste.[12]

INTRODUCING A CHARACTER

When writing a novel a writer should create living people, not characters. A character is a caricature.

~Ernest Hemingway
American Pulitzer and Nobel Prize Winner in Literature

Ernest Hemingway is correct—people should be realistic and believable in a novel. For this study, however, we will use the term "character" since it is widely used in reference to novel writing.

Before characters are actually developed into the manuscript, it is sometimes helpful to write one-page descriptions of the main characters and half-page descriptions of the supportive characters. However, do not limit creativity in writing with those descriptions— the character may change and become someone different as the writing progresses. Character sketches written beforehand are helpful in establishing traits so the actual writing can begin. Think about questions you would like answered about the character and then answer them. By taking the time to write character sketches and descriptions before the writing begins, you will have a better understanding of the part that character will play and how he or she can push the plot forward.

The writer must know the character better than anyone. Practice writing one character as sarcastic, another sweet, another angry, and so on. It also helps to study techniques of great writers—not to copy, but to observe how each character changes in speech. Once a character sketch is finished, you will know better where to insert

12 Jane Austen, *Pride and Prejudice,* Barnes & Noble Classics, New York, 2003 pg. 239.

the character in the setting. Characters may be introduced through dialogue, actions, and internal thoughts through the narrator, revealing what others think about this person. Characters need their own voice because like people, all characters are different.

The following are some ideas for building a character. As stated, do not introduce all there is to know about the character at the beginning. Pick and choose traits as you build the character sketch.

- Physical description: hair color, color and size of eyes (what do the eyes communicate—fear, courage, shyness?) Is the character young, middle-aged, old, short (petite), tall; What about clothes—hip or sloppy?

- Distinguish strong or weak character traits. Person's value system: Is he honest (returns extra change if given too much at the grocery store), a liar, kind, or angry?

- Personality and expressions: scowls a lot, endless energy level, making others tired from her pace, smiles too much, sings all the time, child-like mannerisms, fearful, brave, and so on.

- What does this character think and dream about?

- What do other people think about this person? How do others react to this person?

- Does he stand straight and walk confidently or slump and drag his feet?

- Everyone has something unique about them. How does this character shine? Example: When she smiles, she radiates, putting everyone in a better mood. What are her downfalls?

- What does he do for a living? What is his passion?

- Does she have a pet, a hobby, something she does well? Perhaps she has skill with a sword or an amazing artistic ability.

- What is the character's goal in the story? What is the conflict in the goal? What will this character learn, and how will he change in his circumstances?

- As you write about a character, borrow traits from people you know (the way she rubs her temples when she's frustrated, how her eyes widen in fear, how her face lights up when she sees her dog, and so on).

Using these ideas, a character sketch can be built with confidence. Characters should change and grow, so the protagonists should have flaws. No one is perfect. Some doubt must exist that the main character/s will not have victory—there should always be a challenge to overcome. Characters may fall, but in the end, they should rise and meet the challenge, beating odds to do it. Important to remember is the following: If the good guy is too good, he will not seem real. Leave room for the protagonist to develop.

An example of an antagonist might be that "the villain" is evil, but perhaps he has one good trait. He may have a cat, which is the only living thing to which he gives affection. This could leave room for the villain to change. Of course, some villains are always villains, and they need to stay that way, but do not be timid about characters changing in the story. Write some personal detail, but again the character needs to develop as the story progresses through conflict, actions, and internal thoughts of the character. Keep the reader intrigued.

The introduction of the main character should be memorable. A clear physical image of the person should be written so the readers can picture him or her in their minds right away. Again, a snapshot character sketch is best so readers can gradually grow in their reader relationship with the character. When characters are revealed, readers decide whether they like that person or not at the beginning. Some type of bonding and connection must occur with the reader and character. Why? If readers do not like or at least connect in some way to the main character, why spend three hundred pages reading about him or her?

The following is the memorable introduction of the celebrated character Scarlett O'Hara in the famous novel, *Gone with the Wind*.

> *Scarlett O'Hara was not beautiful, but men seldom realized it when caught by her charm as the Tarleton twins were. In her face were too sharply blended the delicate features of her mother, a Coast aristocrat of French descent, and the heavy ones of her florid Irish father. But it was an arresting face, pointed of chin, square of jaw. Her eyes were pale green without the touch of hazel, starred with bristly black lashes and slightly tilted at the ends. Above them, her thick black brows slanted upward, cutting a startling oblique line in her magnolia-white skin— that skin so prized by Southern women and so carefully guarded with bonnets, veils, and mittens against hot Georgia suns.* [13]

CHOOSING THE NAME OF A CHARACTER

Every writer needs to develop the skill of choosing a fitting name for a character. To choose a character's name, first study names and their meanings. Try several names to see if one fits the character sketch you have written, and see how it works. Think about the syllables, sounds of letters, and how they work together. Try putting different letters, prefixes, and suffixes together to form new names. Zoe was the main character in my book, *The Chosen Path*, and I chose the name Zoe because it means "life." I wanted her to fulfill what her name

13 Margaret Mitchell, *Gone With the Wind*, Pocket Books, New York, London, Toronto, Sydney, 1936, pg. 3.

meant—an extraordinary life. For villains in the story, I studied names and the effect of putting hard sounding letters together (dirt, devil, gall) to form a name that sounded evil and dastardly—Durgalt. A strong supporting character in my book was a prophet named Mahon. Again, I put letters together to form a strong name.

Avoid using similar names in a manuscript. For example, do not use names beginning with the same letter in a scene: Tom, Trevor, Tim—it becomes confusing to the reader, and at the very beginning the reader could forget who is who. Use names with different letters and with a different number of syllables.

DIALECT

After the personality of your character is decided, use words to carefully portray accent and dialect. Characters are revealed not only by what they say, but how they say it. Different parts of a country speak with different dialects, so be sure to study dialect for each character depending on where he or she lives. Speech patterns can be annoying or endearing, so only use dialect when it benefits a character. It can become frustrating for the reader if too many characters have accents and strange speech patterns.

When determining a dialect, think about the personality of the character. For example, if the character has a southern accent, it should be readily understood. Melanie, a Southern belle from Georgia, and Aunt Pitty are supporting characters in *Gone With the Wind*. Their southern dialects are easily recognizable in the following narration.

"I was always so glad dear Papa didn't chew," began Pitty, and Melanie, her frown creasing deeper, swung on her and spoke sharper words than Scarlett had ever heard her speak.

"Oh do hush, Auntie! You're so tactless."

"Oh dear!" Pitty dropped her sewing in her lap and her mouth pursed up in hurt. "I declare. I don't know what ails you all tonight. You and India are just as jumpy and cross as two old sticks."[14]

NARRATOR DEVELOPMENT

The narrator is the storyteller and is the voice that connects with the reader. Invisibility is best in narration. The narrator reveals tidbits of information that might otherwise be difficult for the reader to discover. Narration can help form a connection between the character and reader. The reader should be able to picture scenes and characters vividly through the narrator's voice, but be careful with details—too many can be overwhelming. Build plot through the narrator's voice, and use narration wisely with a balance of narration and dialogue. The narration should be interesting and compelling, honest and authentic, coming in and out of scenes almost unnoticed.

The following is an example of narration from *The Hobbit,* by J.R.R. Tolkien.

With a spring Gollum got up and started shambling off at a great pace. Bilbo hurried after him, still cautiously, though his chief fear now was of tripping on another snag and falling with a noise. His head was in a whirl of hope and wonder. It seemed that the ring he had was a magic ring: it made you invisible! He had heard of such things of course, in old old tales; but it was hard to believe that he really had found one, by accident. Still here it was: Gollum with his bright eyes had passed him by, only a yard to one side.[15]

WRITING DIALOGUE

Writing dialogue can be one of the most difficult writing skills to master. The following is a fine dialogue example in *The Lion, the*

14 Margaret Mitchell, *Gone With the Wind,* Pocket Books, New York, London, Toronto, Sydney, 1936, pg. 1106.

15 J.R.R. Tolkien, *The Hobbit,* Houghton Mifflin Company, Boston, 1937, pg. 78

Witch, and the Wardrobe by C.S. Lewis, from his remarkable, *The Chronicles of Narnia* series.

> *"Good evening, good evening," said the Faun. "Excuse me—I don't want to be inquisitive—but should I be right in thinking that you are a Daughter of Eve?"*
>
> *"My name's Lucy," said she, not quite understanding him.*
>
> *"But you are—forgive me—you are what they call a girl?" asked the Faun.*
>
> *"Of course I'm human," said Lucy, still a little puzzled.*
>
> *"To be sure, to be sure," said the Faun. "How stupid of me! But I've never seen a Son of Adam or a Daughter of Eve before. I am delighted. That is to say—" and then it stopped as if it had been going to say something it had not intended but had remembered in time. "Delighted, delighted," it went on. "Allow me to introduce myself. My name is Tumnus."* [16]

Remember the following in dialogue: 1) use natural speech; 2) avoid having the characters explain what is happening; 3) limit the use of a character's name too often; 4) watch for overuse of modifiers; and 5) create believable characters.

DIALOGUE TIPS

1. **Use natural speech.** Listen carefully to dialogue in movies or television shows. Notice conversations happening around you. You will find that people do not always speak in complete sentences. Dialogue should mimic natural speech. Be careful not to write long paragraphs of dialogue. People do not talk that way.

---

16 C.S. Lewis, *The Lion, the Witch and the Wardrobe,* HarperCollins, New York, 1950, pgs. 11-12.

Dialogue needs to stay natural. People use contractions when they speak—language is not often formal. Write a natural conversation as best you can, and then read it out loud. What you may think looks amazing on paper may sound dull when read out loud. Tape the dialogue and listen to it and see how it can be improved.

When a different character is speaking, begin a new paragraph. This makes the conversation easier to follow. Also, keep the internal thought with that character within the same paragraph.

2. **Avoid having the characters explain what is happening.** For the characters to remain real, they must not explain all the details. Use a narrator if explanation is needed, but do not lecture. If some type of research is important to the story, it is usually best to write it in the narration.

   Practice writing dialogue mixed with narration when a dominant speaker and a listener are in the scene. Add narration when needed, but some things do not need to be written—they are understood. A good writing lesson is to write a narrative using two dominant speakers.

3. **Limit the use of character's names in dialogue.** In natural speech, people's names are not said often. If you think the reader may be in doubt if Mary or John is speaking, use a name then. Once a character has been greeted by name by another character, it should be enough in the dialogue. When switching scenes, characters' names will have to be reintroduced.

4. **Watch for overuse of modifiers.** Do not use the words: *shouted, exclaimed, stated*, and so on. Mark Twain made this statement: "Don't say the old lady screamed—bring her on and let her scream!" *Said* is a word that blends in with novels, but overused it will become a glaring nuisance. Show action; do not tell.

Avoid adverbs (words that end in -*ly*). If the character is angry, then show the action. Instead of writing, "He shouted *angrily*," write, His cup slammed on the table, splashing coffee against the wall. "Get out!" Here is another example: If the new girl in the office trips over her feet and she turns red, it is not necessary to say she was embarrassed.

5. **Create believable characters through dialogue.** The dialogue should be consistent with the character. The highest form of dialogue writing comes when each character has his own particular mannerisms, speech patterns, and actions, and the reader knows right away who is speaking. When this happens, the character becomes real, as if the reader knows the person. However, even when the character is well-known by the reader, remember to use names occasionally to avoid confusion.

Ask others to read the dialogue to see if it is clear. What may seem perfectly clear to the writer may actually be confusing to the reader. Never be overconfident in writing. Every writer needs friends who will be honest and give suggestions.

BLUNDERS IN FICTION WRITING

The following are areas to watch for and improve in writing fiction. With practice, these mistakes can easily be avoided.

1. **Waiting too long to have conflict**—a conflict needs to start at the beginning of the book to draw the reader into the story.

2. **Too many details**—the story should never begin with background information. Background information needs to be dispersed throughout. Too much information at the beginning does not seize the reader's attention. Be careful to include information only if it is relevant to the plot.

Research is important to substantiate material in the manuscript, but be careful not to give too much. Write only what is relevant to the plot. The tendency of some writers is to add too much of what has been researched, just because they have knowledge about a certain subject. Readers will lose contact with the plot and main characters if too much information is given.

3. **Meaningless scenes and details**—do not begin a chapter with someone parking the car, brushing his teeth, and so on. Scenes such as this are mundane and meaningless. Everyone has to sleep—it is understood. Do not waste dialogue with such greetings as: "How are you?" "I'm fine." It is boring. Unless it is important to the plot, limit such scenes.

   Do not give names and information about characters who have tiny parts. Descriptions should only be given to important and supportive characters.

4. **Summarizing ten years of someone's life in a few sentences**—a couple of sentences cannot begin to pull the weight of all that has happened to a main character in ten years. If a certain part of someone's life needs to be known, use flashback, or write a conversation between two characters, exposing important details necessary to the plot.

5. **Boring language**—choose words carefully. Use language in the most beneficial way with intrigue and imagination. Avoid clichés—"hard as a rock," "cold as ice," "cuddly as a kitten," "burst out laughing," and so on. Clichés weaken writing. Find unique ways to say what is obvious if it is important. Use bold imagery to equal the character and scenery. If a character is depressed, do not say it—show it. Create the imagery of her sitting in a room with the lights off and the shades down, staring. Learn to put pictures into words.

6. **Sudden happenings**—do not switch scenes too quickly. Use transitions to switch places. For example, if a character is taking a walk, she should not suddenly answer a phone inside. Use some type of shift between scenes that will enable the plot to flow and seem real.

7. **Too many coincidences**—coincidences may work in the beginning, but it is harder to write in the end. Sometimes writers will use a coincidence because it can make the writing easier. Be careful because this will weaken the story. Characters need to be responsible for their actions.

8. **Not enough environment**—characters need to have some type of environment—everyone has a home, work, etc. Give readers a sense of where a character lives, his habits, where he works, what he does for fun, and his purpose.

9. **Poor pace to the story**—a strong beginning and ending are necessary, but the middle of the book needs to move along as well. If you find there is not enough pace in your story, take out every unnecessary scene—if it does not advance the plot, it should not be there. Add something new and fresh in the middle. Keep a pace that intrigues—conflict, calm, fun, more excitement, tension, peace until the story resolves. Pace is one of the most challenging parts of writing. Ask others to read your manuscript, specifically looking at the pace to see where the manuscript could be improved.

10. **Keep an element of surprise**—do not give away a big scene that is about to happen. Stories should have some tension, but it is also important to have times of peace, time to breathe and enjoy. Too much sadness without moments of joy can be depressing to the reader. Hold back some information for intrigue, but add it before the plot becomes too frustrating.

CONCLUSION IN NOVELS

Be careful not to cut the ending short. Readers wait and wait for the climax in the book, and if very little is written at the end, it becomes frustrating to the reader. Make the reading memorable. Give the reader the reward for reading your book.

In the conclusion, all loose ends must be tied. Do not leave questions unanswered. Make the ending fit with the context of the story. In the last couple of pages, there should be a hint as to the future of the main characters. All conclusions do not necessarily have to end "happily ever after," but the ending does need to be satisfying. The reader will take that ending and visualize all kinds of possibilities. If you think you might want to write a sequel, create a hook so readers will want to read the next book.

Writing is rewriting. A writer must learn to deepen characters, trim writing, intensify scenes. To fall in love with the first draft to the point where one cannot change it is to greatly enhance the prospects of never publishing.

~Richard North Patterson
Novelist

SPECIFIC EDITS FOR FICTION

Plan on spending a lot of time editing fiction. Specific edits are included in this section to help with making your manuscript tighter. Mark any of these to change later:

- Is your point of view (first, second, or third person) consistent?

- Review the first part of the book again and be certain that it is strong. Does the first sentence and paragraph draw interest? Remember, you must grab the reader's attention immediately.

- Is the rest of the chapter attention grabbing?

- Perhaps a plot did not unfold correctly because an important part was missing. Mark those parts.

- Check to be sure that all main characters have been described. Readers must have a picture of characters when they are introduced. Are characters stated in a positive form—who they are, rather than who they are not? Check for the negative words of no and not. State what is, rather than what is not.

- Once characters have been physically described during their introduction, they should not be described again. If you have a reason for adding some description again (and it should be instrumental to the plot), do it in a different way. Perhaps a new twist with the character needs to be inserted in the story. Also, check to make sure the physical descriptions of characters do not change in the manuscript.

- Personality traits should be revealed throughout the book as the character is revealed and changes.

- Look at the character's emotions—are they too strong or too weak? Adjust as necessary.

- Check for changes in names during your edit. During an edit of *The Chosen Path*, I discovered that I had not changed a name of a character at the end of the book that I renamed in the beginning. Thankfully, I caught the error, and it was corrected before printing. Be consistent with character names.

- Do some characters wander into the story and then leave, contributing very little to the story? Delete those characters. When a part does not serve to enhance the story, take it out.

- Check the dialogue by reading it out loud. Does it sound real? Does the dialogue fit the character? The dialogue may need to be spiced up or slowed down. By reading dialogue out loud, you will discover if it seems real or not.

- Check to make certain that each new speaker begins a new paragraph.

- Check for long paragraphs of dialogue. People do not usually speak for the length of a long paragraph, so add some action in between dialogue if needed. Look for and delete dialogue descriptions before a speaker such as the following: He exclaimed; she smiled. Look for boring sections and delete those. Use action to show emotion instead.

- Is there enough description in the scenes? Change any monotonous scenes. Make sure there is rhythm.

- Are too many adjectives used? Look for -*ly* adverbs—change to action.

- Do scenes jump in time? Keep the time in a scene logical. Unless it is important to the plot, do not jump back and forth in years. Does the plot consistently move along?

- During the initial read-through, make sure the novel is unraveling the way it was intended.

- Look for smooth transitions. Check for missing parts that could confuse the reader.

- Look for your favorite shining parts in the book. What made them great? My suggestion is to rewrite other sections that are not up to that standard.

- Replace overused phrases and clichés with wording that is new and fresh.

- Finally, does the story make sense? Are loose ends tied up? Is the ending memorable?

- Ask several honest and candid people to read your manuscript and to note where they wanted more or less in the story. If it is consistently the same, you need to work on those parts. A manuscript does not need to be read just once by the writer and a friend, but MANY times, and in turn it will need MANY edits.

Once the manuscript is finished, there may be a premature urge to ship it to a publisher. Do not do this. A polished manuscript can mean the difference between a fair and an outstanding manuscript and the rejection or acceptance for publication. Careful editing is what makes a manuscript shine. Editing is a crucial step in the completion of all writing. Take time to study and implement editing skills to make your fictional writing the best it can be.

WORD COUNTS FOR FICTION

Word counts vary by types of fiction. Most publishing companies have their own guidelines, so be sure to contact them. The following is a general guide to word counts for fiction.

MICRO-FICTION

Typically, micro-fiction is less than 400 words. Micro-fiction is popular in magazines because it is a condensed story that takes little room. Every word will need to count in micro-fiction, with the essential use of colorful and stirring words. Something must be discovered and solved in a brief amount of space. Many edits and re-edits will need to transpire to make it as tight and exciting as possible.

FLASH FICTION

Flash fiction is short work from 300–1,000 words. Flash fiction is usually a single act or part of a multifaceted subject. With such a small word count, it must be action-packed and begin immediately. One dominant character should be the focus with a potent twist at the end.

SHORT STORY

A short story is a fictional description of an event or events usually in anthologies or periodicals. The word count is generally from 1,000–7,500 words. Short stories are to the point, typically with one or two main characters that face a conflict or event. Short stories can usually be read in one sitting.

NOVELETTE

A novelette is typically a light, romantic story that is sentimental. The word count for a novelette is typically from 7,500–20,000. Many publishers are hesitant to print a novelette because the length is too long to use in a magazine, but not long enough for a novel.

NOVELLA

Most novellas are young adult fiction and romance genres, divided into chapters and are usually printed in the smaller, mass market size. The word count for a novella is from 20,000–50,000 words.

NOVEL

A novel is a fictional work, frequently with a complex plot, and it is divided into chapters. The story usually develops through the feelings, views, and actions of the characters. Fiction genres are varied and so is their word count, but they generally have a word count from

60,000–110,000. For a first novel, it is best to keep the word count between 60,000–70,000. Publishers may be hesitant to spend money on a book much longer than this because they are taking a chance if the author is unknown.

WORD COUNTS FOR MISCELLANEOUS FICTIONAL CATEGORIES

Contemporary romance: 60,000–80,000

Mystery: 60,000–80,000

Science-Fiction/Fantasy: 80,000–120,000

Thriller: 90,000–120,000

Historical Romance: 100,000–125,000

Fictional works with a word count of 125,000–150,000 and up will most likely need to be broken into a series. The attention spans of most people will not allow them to read a book of this length. Also, it becomes difficult for a writer to make a plot flow and be exciting with that many words.

No tears in the writer, no tears in the reader. No surprise in the writer, no surprise in the reader.

~Robert Frost

CHAPTER ELEVEN

ESPECIALLY FOR NON-FICTION WRITERS

Words—so innocent and powerless as they are, as standing in a dictionary, how potent for good and evil they become in the hands of one who knows how to combine them.

~Nathaniel Hawthorne
American novelist

WHAT IS NON-FICTION?

Non-fiction is writing true and factual information about actual lives or events. Non-fiction writing can be just as creative as fictional writing, if the author perseveres to find a creative angle. Creative non-fiction, which combines the elements of both fiction and non-fiction, giving the best of both, is becoming a new genre in children's and adult's writing. Anyone can tell facts, but why is it important to write about them? The material should be relevant and useful while answering important questions. Humor added to non-fiction writing will take out some of the dryness of facts. As with any genre of writing, a target audience must be decided before the writing begins.

Dialogue or quotes can be used to enliven non-fiction work. Many journalists use this technique at the beginning of an article for effect. Dialogue or quotes can give emotional impact and life to an article. For instruction on how to write dialogue and other techniques in writing, refer to Chapter Ten, "Especially for Fiction Writers."

Writing a back cover before you begin writing your manuscript can be helpful. Back covers typically summarize a book with wording that draws attention. Because of the limited space, every word on the back cover must be powerful. Of course, you will probably rewrite the actual back cover before it is published, but this will help you to stay on course with the theme and significance of the book when writing.

TYPES OF NON-FICTION WRITING

Non-fiction writing includes biography, autobiography, scientific writing, textbook, history, travel writing, personal journaling, and "how-to" books (cookbooks, gardening, decorating, carpentry, etc.). Also included are journalism/media for newspaper and magazine articles, sermons, speeches, as well as advertising, posters, and leaflets. The following are overviews of some genres in non-fiction.

BIOGRAPHY

A biography is the story of someone's life, written by another person. Biographies are not only fun to write, but people love human interest stories. A biography should showcase the person's life and the influence the person had—his or her legacy. To include every aspect of someone's life is difficult, so using an angle or slant in the story will add depth and focus to the writing.

If the person is still alive, interviews are the best way to discover information, which will be an added bonus to the writing. Other sources of information include the following: notes from a diary, letters, newspaper articles, other biographies, and reference books (including encyclopedias and articles on the Internet). The following should be researched: date and place of birth and death, family facts such as siblings, housing, and life as a child, education, other achievements, defining moments in life, obstacles that were overcome, major events, and impact on others.

A biography does not have to be about a famous person. When normal people have meaningful lives and accomplish extraordinary things, most people want to read about it. Those who overcome adversity are an inspiration to many. People want to read about those who have succeeded in life—it gives them hope that they can do the same.

If the biography is about someone who has died, be sure to enliven the story by adding something personal about him or her—perhaps a humorous habit, a favorite hobby, or something unique. For example, President John Quincy Adams had a strange pet, an alligator, which was kept in the East Room of the White House. I wonder how many maids stayed in their positions while he was President? He was the sixth President and son to John Adams, second President, which explains why Quincy must always be added to distinguish his name from his father's. Find information that is unique about the person and disperse it throughout the writing to add interest. Also, consider searching for living relatives who could provide a vast source of information about the person.

I have written a number of biographies as articles, six of which were compiled into my second book, *Pathway to Purpose.* I wrote about each person from a different angle. For example, after researching Charles M. Schulz' life, I wrote from the angle that he was an overcomer in life. The following is the first paragraph:

Charles M. Schulz was an overcomer. His past did not hinder his future—it propelled him into his lifelong profession as a cartoonist. As we reflect upon his life, we will see how he overcame what may seem to have been shortcomings to launch himself into a victorious life.

Another example of a remarkable person I wrote about was Harriet Tubman. She was a famous conductor in the Underground Railroad, freeing more than three hundred slaves, including herself. I wrote the article from the angle of her courage. I picked examples from her life to make my point, while adding some personality traits I discovered about her. I also included quotes that helped to add interest to her story.

In a biographical book, an author has more room to expand about a person, giving details that could never be written in an article. However, even when writing a book, it is still more powerful to stay with an angle—the significant factor in a person's life which made him or her extraordinary.

The most important key to writing a biography is to make sure all the facts are true about the person. Research the research to ensure that what is being written actually happened in a person's life. Write about defining moments—events in the person's life that shaped them into who they became. Write about lifetime accomplishments and how they affected others. As a result, was there any historical significance? Leave the reader with something memorable about the person. It can be difficult to be objective when you are composing a biography, but it is important to make sure that everything written can be supported, thus making the biography a work of truth and enlightenment about the person.

Biographies have the tendency to be overflowing with facts, so to make them more palatable, it is helpful to add suspense and humor, just like real life. Keep the writing fresh and lively. Do not simply list names, dates, and events in a long, boring list. Place of birth and death, and family information is helpful, but do not begin a biography with those facts. Begin with something interesting, motivating, but relevant. For example, if the biography is about Johnny Cash, it would be a good idea to relate something strategic that happened the year he was born, which later affected him or was a defining moment in his life. In 1932, the same year Johnny Cash was born, Radio City Music Hall opened—where he would later perform one of his most moving performances. It will take time to discover facts like this, but it will make the biography intriguing, which will keep readers reading. If you are writing about how Johnny Cash overcame his past, add quotes that can support that angle such as the following:

You build on failure. You use it as a stepping stone. Close the door on the past. You don't try to forget the mistakes, but you don't dwell on it. You don't let it have any of your energy, or any of your time, or any of your space.

~Johnny Cash
Grammy Award-winning singer/songwriter

Add your own opinions, observations, and conclusions, but notate them as such. Be sure not to distort facts or make unfounded accusations. If other biographies are written on your subject, read them. Include excerpts from them to help back up different points being made about the person's life you are sketching. Support your opinions with examples and facts. I cannot stress enough the importance of research. Research not only adds exciting reality to your manuscript, but it brings credibility to your writing. Always use footnotes when using quotes. This will bring validity to the biography you are writing.

AUTOBIOGRAPHY

An autobiography is the author telling his or her own story, perhaps as a memoir. Written in first person, the author has the advantage of telling how he or she felt when certain incidences happened in life. The writer needs to think about defining moments—what must be shared so that others may learn from them. Many people write autobiographies from personal journals (see the section below on journaling). Journaling experiences in life are an enlightening way to chronicle memories that are just too important to forget. Even if the autobiography is never published, writing about your life will be a treasure to your children, grandchildren, and those born long after you have left this world. Keeping a journal will make writing an autobiography far easier.

PERSONAL JOURNALING

Personal journaling is a writing of events, expressions, emotions, and experiences that are usually written for private use by the writer. Journaling is either handwritten in a book or typed on a computer. Some people find journaling helpful in identifying hopes, dreams, goals, or even fears that need to be overcome. Entries should be dated, and logged where it is written if the place is significant.

Some personal journals are written to be handed down to family members. Histories of families can be included so they will not be forgotten. Children in the family will benefit from learning about how life was in a time before them. Family trees can be included. Humorous, interesting, historic, and special stories and traditions are wonderful additions to a personal journal. The wisdom learned through life's successes and failures can help those in future generations. If the writer has strong religious views, a personal journal is a good place to express those. Observations and pictures of family members can be included. Treasured family recipes can be added for families to enjoy. Avid readers may want to make notes of outstanding books for others in their family to later read. The list of types of journal entries can go on and on. A life well-lived will not be easily forgotten—especially if written in a journal for others to treasure.

If you write in a personal journal, try writing the entry on another piece of paper or on a computer and then edit it so the writing is clear and crisp. This is one of the best ways to improve your writing daily. You may be surprised just how many words can be deleted to make the writing stronger and more effective.

Although few personal journals are written with the intention of being published, the possibility exists of them being published later as a memoir or autobiography. Some personal journals of extraordinary people have been discovered and published after a person has died, especially those of great historical and literary interest. *Anne Frank: The Diary of a Young Girl*, chronicles the life of Anne and her family during World War II (June 12, 1942–August 1, 1944). From the pen of Anne Frank in the outlet of her diary, flowed her deepest thoughts during a traumatic time of her short life, her family, and others during the Holocaust.

Lewis Carroll, famous for writing *Alice's Adventures in Wonderland*, wrote several diaries, but a few are missing (from 1858–1862). Some think his family wanted to hide personal information. Journals can become too personal, depending on how much the writer wants to disclose about his or her life. Be careful what is written. Sometimes it helps to explore feelings through a journal, but remember, when you have passed from this life, someone is most likely going to read it. Be sure what you have written is something you want your family or friends to know.

JOURNALISM

Journalism is the profession of reporting or publishing timely, factual events locally, nationally, or internationally. Journalism is multi-faceted and includes many areas of expertise. Although a specific degree in journalism is not mandatory, from my research on journalism, a degree is helpful, especially if the study is in a particular field in journalism. A communication degree is helpful if television or radio journalism is a preference. Photography skills are of course necessary for a photojournalist. An English degree will help in all aspects of writing journalism, so choose what best suits your chosen profession and take the needed classes.

If you are undecided about the field of journalism for a profession, take classes in different types of journalism so that you can narrow down which type is your passion. Branches of journalism include the following: newspaper, magazine, investigative, photo, food, music, radio, television, and online, with each type having specific skills that need to be learned for that type of media. The following, however, are basic journalism skills.

1. Research skills are essential for accurate writing. A journalist needs to acquire facts on the subject, confirm those facts, and then report them truthfully.

2. Writing skills are vital in news and feature stories in magazines and periodicals. Learning how to put the punch in titles and articles is fundamental to writing journalism. Good spelling, grammar, and punctuation are basic skills that need to be learned. A clear, creative, easy to understand ability in writing is necessary.

3. Communication skills—journalists need communication skills for interviewing, as well as the quickness of asking probing questions that will render informative answers. A reporter will need to go to the location where the news is happening to get accurate information. Listening skills enable a journalist to formulate questions during the interview. Through interviews, a reporter will typically ask the questions: who, what, when, where, why, and

how. Good people skills are necessary for an interview—no one likes to answer questions from someone who is overbearing and obnoxious. Journalists also need to have tact with sensitive questions, and a sense of humor always helps to make the interview more relaxing. Last, a journalist needs to be trustworthy—if he says he will not use confidential information, he should not.

4. Editing skills—the better the article is written, the less work editors will have to do. In some small newspapers, the journalist may have to not only be the writer but the editor as well. Take time to learn the essential skills needed to write and edit well.

5. Photography skills—multi-tasking is advantageous in journalism. The old saying, "a picture is worth a thousand words," never fit better than photography in journalism. Pictures can add just the right zest to a well-written story. Photo composition, timing, and digital photography are important to know. Carry a camera at all times—photo opportunities happen randomly.

6. HTML (hyper text markup language) is a computer language used for website creation. Many journalism writing jobs in the future will be online, so it is important to know something about text formatting for websites.

7. Perseverance and initiative—necessary skills for every writer. If a reporter wants a story, it takes perseverance to get that story. A journalist who has initiative will be looking for stories, rather than waiting for something to happen.

Taking classes will definitely help in learning journalism skills, but applying the skills in an internship will further the skills even more. One of the best teachers is experience, especially in journalism. During an internship, editors/supervisors realize that the intern is learning, and there may be some grace at the beginning to make a few mistakes, but not for long. By interning, later jobs may open up from that experience.

A journalism career is fast-paced because every journalist is trying to be one step ahead of the other—to get top headlines. The reporting should not be biased but factual, which is not always the case. The editorial section in the newspaper is devoted to writing opinions; articles should be facts. Sometimes in newspaper articles, exaggeration can occur to make the story more interesting. A selective use of facts can distort the truth as well. A writer's perception can sway readers to a distorted truth. When that happens and the distortion is discovered, the integrity of the journalist will be compromised. It is extremely important to write the truth—do not add or take away from what truly happened. Do not be too quick to report a headline. Some newspapers go ahead with a news breaking headline and article to draw attention, knowing that the next day a retraction can be placed (most of the retractions are not placed where people will see them). Speculation is not truth; it is best to wait and get the complete story. Truth is unvarying, and it should be reported as so.

A photograph can distort the truth as well. Pictures do not lie, so be certain that the assumption from the picture will reveal the truth. For example, a movie star may kiss a friend on the cheek goodbye, but the caption may say that she now has a new boyfriend. Wrong conclusions will be surmised if inaccurate captions are given.

Truthful journalism is informative. A journalist has the choice of projecting light or darkness. Bad things do happen, and people need to be informed, but encouraging things also happen in life. Writing can come through the eyes of despair or the eyes of hope. Stories should be written with integrity and wisdom. When that occurs, credibility and respect for that journalist will grow.

TRAVEL WRITING

Obviously, the best way to write about a chosen destination is to go there. Planning needs to take place before the trip. Research the history, culture, and sights, making a list of places to visit. Study a map and become familiar with the town or country. Read articles and books about the area to see what has been written previously so those ideas will not be repeated. The more that is known about the destination beforehand, the more fruitful and enjoyable the trip will be. If it is a foreign destination, knowing the language will be a plus, but even if the language is not known, at least learn some essential phrases and buy a language translation book to have on hand. Take a digital camera to capture the people, culture, food, and beauty of the land. Experiment with shots of people, places up close and far away, monuments, festivals, flowers, beaches, homes of celebrated artists, historical sites, and mountains—anything that has appeal.

Writing about travel becomes unique when it is written from the writer's perspective. When the travel destination is reached, immediately begin to watch and listen to all that is happening. Travel writing should be written through the experience of the five senses—the tastes of the local restaurant, what home is like in a small community, the rich feel of the land, the joy of a hometown wedding, the smell of the city, and any unusual characters.

Talk to people in the area and take a glimpse of their daily lives. If you happen upon someone who is excited about the area, hidden treasures may be discovered, igniting fresh ideas for a story. Find out what is special about the city—the best places to eat, visit, and experience. Getting to know some locals may bring an invitation to a home-cooked meal. If the food is amazing, ask for a recipe or two to be included in the writing. Search out and find the best and worst of the city—hotels, restaurants, museums, churches, and other attractions, but try to accentuate the positive, not the negative. After all, you want people to actually visit the destination. Keep all brochures, advertisements, ticket stubs, maps of the area, and odds and ends picked up in your journey. These could be used in writing and the layout or cover of the book.

Experiences need to be written in a travel journal as they happen, not after time has lapsed. Otherwise, much will be forgotten. Try to write down conversations with the locals because dialogue makes the writing more vibrant. Capture any sensation or impression that is unique. Take as many notes as possible so a large amount of material will be available to use later. If excitement was experienced at the destination, capture that excitement in the writing. Excitement is contagious, which is what travel writers want readers to experience when reading about the destination.

When you finally arrive home, start writing as soon as possible—capture the enthusiasm of the journey while it is still fresh. Begin with the first impression of the destination (which should be written in your travel journal). Write for someone who has never experienced the place—all that made it amazing. Add humor, bold phrases, and picturesque words to capture the heart of the destination. As with any writing, begin with a hook—something to capture attention right away and keep it exciting throughout; then end with a bang. Travel writing can be surprisingly creative through the use of imagery and the telling of personal experiences. When readers feel like they have experienced what was written, the article or book is a success.

RESEARCH, OUTLINE, AND WRITING NON-FICTION

When writing non-fiction, research more than the amount of material that could be used in the writing. Having more than what is needed will save time and interruption later in researching for more. Organize the research by topics, either in an outline or on cards. Later, that material can be separated into chapters.

Using an outline in non-fiction writing is beneficial. List major points to be covered. The advantage of an outline is to help stay on track, which will keep the writing clear and easy to follow. The reader must follow the development of points to fully benefit from the writing.

As with any type of writing, a hook must be established at the beginning of the book to entice the reader to keep reading. When writing about a specific topic in non-fiction, be careful to stay away from jargon of the topic or field. You may be an expert about a certain topic, and peers could benefit from your research, but the average person who is trying to learn from your writing will be lost. Using perplexing words only brings frustration to those who do not understand the topic. This does not mean you have to write too simply, but it does mean that complex issues should be written clearly for the general reader.

Editing and proofreading are the final parts of all writing. The manuscript or article needs to be grammatically correct and error free in punctuation and spelling. Do not be slack in editing and proofreading.

NON-FICTION WORD COUNTS

Generally, non-fiction books have a shorter word count than fiction, though they may have the same amount of pages, due to illustrations or pictures added. The minimum word count for a non-fiction book is 25,000 words, which will fill a thin, mass market paperback. Depending on the type of non-fiction, such as textbooks, it could be 200,000 words or more. Of course, some types of picture books can be non-fiction as well, so the word counts will be considerably smaller for a children's target audience. The average word count for an adult non-fiction book is approximately 70,000–80,000. In researching word count for non-fiction, I discovered that some publishing companies will not accept any manuscript above 90,000 words. Check with specific publishing companies because word counts will vary.

WORD COUNTS FOR MISCELLANEOUS NON-FICTION GENRES

Biography: 50,000–90,000

Autobiography: 50,000–90,000

Business and "How-to" books: 50,000–70,000 words

Journalism: Newspaper articles are typically 1,200 words or less, depending upon the space in the newspaper. Articles in periodicals have approximately a 2,000 word count but can be larger if permitted by publisher.

...I feel that every time I write a page either of prose or of verse, with real effort, even if it's thrown into the fire the next minute, I am so much further on.[17]

~C.S. Lewis

17 Wayne Martindale and Jerry Root, *The Quotable Lewis,* Tyndale House Publishers, Wheaton, 1990, pg. 622, quote from: *The Letters of C.S. Lewis to Arthur Greeves,* pgs. 109-110.

CHAPTER TWELVE

ESPECIALLY FOR WRITERS OF POETRY

There are three things, after all, that a poem must reach: the eye, the ear, and what we may call the heart or the mind. It is most important of all to reach the heart of the reader.

~Robert Frost, American poet

Though poetry and songwriting are different, this chapter may also help songwriters develop their lyrics because songs, like poetry, can awaken intense and deep emotions through words. C.S. Lewis commented: "Poetry most often communicates emotions, not directly, but by creating imaginatively the grounds for those emotions. It therefore communicates something more than emotion; only by means of that something more does it communicate the emotions at all."[18]

Perhaps in no other forms of writing, poetry and lyrics can bring a reader to the greatest heights of hope and encouragement or transfer a reader or listener to the depths of despair and discouragement. Carefully written, words can change one's outlook. Samuel Johnson,

---

18 Wayne Martindale and Jerry Root, *The Quotable Lewis,* Tyndale House Publishers, Wheaton, 1990, pg. 476, quoted from *Reflections on the Psalms, pg. 5.*

English author and poet said, "Poetry is the art of uniting pleasure with truth."

Most treasure is found buried deep under the ground. Likewise, digging deep will loosen what the heart wants to say within the poet. Once the heart of the poet connects with a theme, it will transfer into what needs to be said through the carrier of his or her words. Many times a moral purpose is used by the poet to persuade the reader, but universally, all poets begin with some type of inspiration as the starting point. In quiet and reflection, poetry is birthed. The English poet, William Wordsworth, said: "Poetry is the spontaneous overflow of powerful feelings: it takes its origin from emotion recollected in tranquility."

Opening words in the poem lay a path for the reader to find. As the poetry moves forward, the reader follows by interpreting the meaning. The poet hopes that the reader will follow the path being laid, but that is not always the case. Readers will glean from what they find. One verse may have more meaning to a reader and thereafter guide the focus of the rest of the poetry. Another person may find a different meaning. The more a poem is read, the more layers of meaning will be discovered. Poetry is music to those who comprehend the words, which adds to the beauty and joy of the interpretation. C.S. Lewis, in *A Preface to Paradise Lost,* wrote: "Every poem can be considered in two ways—as what the poet has to say, and as a thing which he makes."

THE SOUND OF WORDS

The beauty of words lies in the reflection it gives to those who read or hear them. Some words may evoke a memory and will be interpreted as joyful, painful, life-changing, hopeful, and so on. Some words may have a light or dark sound to them. For example, when I hear the word "spray," I think about ocean spray as I walk along a seashore. That word may have a different meaning for someone else. By maneuvering words with particular sounds, the reader can experience many reactions.

An effective way to exercise using the sound of words and their meanings is to write separate lists of words that you like and dislike. On one list, write words that have pleasant sounds, interesting meanings, or bring a joyful picture to mind. On the other list, write words that feel gloomy, distressing, and sad. Say the words out loud and listen to the sounds they make. What feelings arise when you say them? Keep pages in a writing journal where you can write words that are your favorites or have a particular feeling—good or bad. Another idea is to use a thesaurus and look up the meaning of all the words on your list. Record those as well in your writing journal. Keep adding words to the list because favorite ones can quickly become overused. Categorize them, and when you have a list of words, move them around in a different order to hear and feel what is communicated. Robert Frost once said, "Poetry is when an emotion has found its thought and the thought has found words." Words evoke emotions by the perspective the reader discovers through them.

BASIC POETRY TERMS

Poetry is the most condensed form of literature, so to understand the vast subject, an in-depth study is needed. One large book cannot contain all there is to know about poetry because there is so much to learn. If you are an aspiring poet, read and study the many aspects of poetry. The following is a simple overview of some basic poetry terms that will help you to get started.

Audience—the audience is the person or people whom the speaker of the poem is addressing which could be the reader, another character in the poem, or someone not present.

Diction—the carefully chosen words by the poet that relate meaning and sound, providing the tone and feeling of the poem. *Denotation:* using words according to dictionary meaning. *Connotation:* using words according to the negative, positive, or neutral emotions from the thought or idea associated with that word.

Imagery—Words creatively used can arouse any or all of the five senses: hearing, seeing, feeling, tasting, and smelling. Use words that are concrete, tangible. Think about these words: *Whispering winds stretched through the rocks, misting her trembling lips with salt.* All five senses are experienced in that one line. An emotion of joy could be the theme of another verse as with the following: Laughter arose as each effervescent wave inched closer. Reflect on the poetic imagery in the following excerpt from a poem written by Emily Dickinson, a major American poet.

Hope

Hope is a thing with feathers
That perches in the soul,
And sings the tune without words
And never stops at all.

Irony—one meaning is stated, but an opposite meaning is intended. The way something appears can be the opposite of what is true. Irony in poetry is indirect—not stating what is. It could be that an action caused the reverse of what was expected. The following is an excerpt of an irony poem by Samuel Taylor Coleridge (1772–1834), English poet and philosopher. Water quenches thirst, yet in the poem, none is drinkable.

The Rime of the Ancient Mariner

Water, water, every where,
And all the boards did shrink;
Water, water, every where,
Nor any drop to drink.

Metaphor—uses a word or phrase to imply (though not literally) a similarity to another word or phrase. Metaphors are generally not related but designate one thing for another. The words *as* or *like* are not used in the comparison. Metaphors can add depth and interest with just a few words, adding layers of meaning and a better understanding of what has been written. Orson Scott Card, American novelist said: "Metaphors have a way of holding the most truth in the least space." The following are examples of metaphors: "I am the Bread of Life" (Jesus); life is a journey of challenges; and a dream goes beyond the corners of logic.

Psalm 23, with its beautiful metaphorical comparison between the Lord and a shepherd, is one of the most beloved Psalms in the Bible. The nature of a shepherd is to protect his sheep with great care, just as the Lord protects His people. In this Psalm, the Lord, as a Shepherd, brings peace, guidance, restoration, comfort, and mercy, just as a shepherd would care for his sheep.

Psalm 23

The LORD is my shepherd;
I shall not want.
He makes me to lie down in green pastures;
He leads me beside the still waters.
He restores my soul;
He leads me in the paths of righteousness
for His name's sake.

Yea, though I walk through the valley of the shadow of death,
I will fear no evil;
For You are with me;
Your rod and Your staff, they comfort me.

You prepare a table before me in the presence of my enemies;
You anoint my head with oil;
My cup runs over.

Surely goodness and mercy shall follow me
All the days of my life;
And I will dwell in the house of the LORD
Forever (NKJV).

Goal—as with any writing, poetry must have a goal. What is the purpose?

Meter—a pattern of stressed (accented or long) and unstressed (unaccented or short) syllables that recurs in the lines of poetry

Mood—the atmosphere of the poem that is conveyed. Mood is expressed through the use of imagery in words and the choice or choices of the following: figurative words, symbolism, dialect, use of the five senses, punctuation, or length of stanzas. Reflect upon the mood of the following poem.

Snow flakes
Emily Dickinson

Snow flakes.
I counted till they danced so
Their slippers leaped the town,
And then I took a pencil
To note the rebels down.
And then they grew so jolly
I did resign the prig,
And ten of my once stately toes
Are marshalled for a jig!

Oxymoron—a form of paradox when two opposite or contradictory terms are combined together. The following are examples: definite maybe, clearly confused, darkly lit, same difference, extinct life, unbiased opinion, original copy, genuine imitation, rolling stop, minor crisis, deafening silence, found missing, open secret, clearly confused, almost exactly, and so on. Alfred Tennyson (1809-1892), English poet, wrote the poem *Idylls of the King*. The following line from that poem contains two oxymorons: "And **faith unfaithful** kept him **falsely true.**"

Paradox—has Greek origin: *para* means "aside from, contrary" and *doxa* "opinion;" so putting it together, paradox means "aside from and contrary (opposing) opinion." In poetry, a paradox gives tension by stating something that may go against common sense but is true. John Donne (1572–1631), metaphysical poet, priest, and writer, wrote a paradox in his famous poem, *Death, Be Not Proud*. He explained that death has nothing to be proud of because in the end, death has no power. Death itself is defeated by those who have received salvation because they go on to live eternal bliss in heaven. Donne was a deeply religious man who wrote about death to ease the people's fears. Donne's poem is based on I Corinthians 15:51-57.

Death Be Not Proud

DEATH, be not proud, though some have called thee
Mighty and dreadful, for thou art not so:
For those whom thou think'st thou dost overthrow
Die not, poor Death; nor yet canst thou kill me.
Much pleasure, then from thee much more must flow;
And soonest our best men with thee do go—
Rest of their bones and souls' delivery!
Thou'rt slave to fate, chance, kings, and desperate men,
And dost with poison, war, and sickness dwell;

> And poppy or charms can make us sleep as well
> And better than thy stroke. Why swell'st thou then?
> One short sleep past, we wake eternally,
> And Death shall be no more: Death, thou shalt die!

Rhyme—the repetition of identical vowel and consonant sounds in two or more words: plea, flee; cry, lie; long, song. Rhyme can occur in different types of sequences—not just AABB as below in Shel Silverstein's poem. Rhyme can be arranged in any number of sequences within the lines.

Rhyme pattern—is the pattern established by using the last words in two or more lines which rhyme in a stanza or poem. Shel Silverstein (1930-1999) was an American poet, among many of his talents. The following example is the first four lines from Silverstein's, *Cloony the Clown.*

> I'll tell you the story of Cloony the Clown
> Who worked in a circus that came through town.
> His shoes were too big and his hat was too small,
> But he just wasn't, just wasn't funny at all.

Rhythm—the actual repetition and organization of stress within a poem. Stress is the emphasis that occurs on some syllables but not on others.

Simile—stated so one object is similar to another. Simile uses the words *as* and *like* or *appears* and *seems* to show similarity. The following are examples of similes: the sea is clear as glass; warm like a thick, soft blanket; an unfulfilled dream like a discarded gift. Robert Burns, Scottish poet (1759-1796), was famous for bringing sentimentality to Scottish poetry. The following excerpt from his poem, "A Red, Red Rose," is an example of simile:

My love is like a red, red rose
That's newly sprung in June:
My love is like the melody
That's sweetly played in tune.
As fair art thou, my bonnie lass,
So deep in love am I:
And I will love thee still, my dear,
Till a' the seas gang dry.

Speaker—the person who the reader is imagining is speaking. The poet may or not be the speaker. If the poet is not the speaker, a character is created called *the persona.* The poet imagines that he or she is another person and writes from that perspective. When one person is used to narrate the whole poem, it is called *dramatic monologue.* This type of poetry may sound like a one-sided conversation.

Subject—what the poem is about (general topic). Pinpointing the subject is the first step in writing a poem. Is the poem about nature, an emotion, God, ecology, how to make a difference, love, and so on?

Symbolism—a visible expression used to imply more than its literal meaning, representing a concept or an idea. Objects, places, or things are used in symbolism to deepen and expand the words of the poet, who is counting on the reader to understand the meaning. Robert Frost (1874–1963), popular twentieth-century American poet, wrote the following poem in 1916. Some interpret the poem literally (inspirationally) while others consider it to have an ironic interpretation. That is the beauty of poetry—the symbolism can be interpreted in so many ways. Frost even made a warning about his poem: "You have to be careful of that one; it's a tricky poem—very tricky."

The Road Not Taken

Two roads diverged in a yellow wood,
And sorry I could not travel both
And be one traveler, long I stood
And looked down one as far as I could
To where it bent in the undergrowth;
Then took the other, as just as fair,
And having perhaps the better claim,
Because it was grassy and wanted wear;
Though as for that the passing there
Had worn them really about the same,

And both that morning equally lay
In leaves no step had trodden black.
Oh, I kept the first for another day!
Yet knowing how way leads on to way,
I doubted if I should ever come back.

I shall be telling this with a sigh
Somewhere ages and ages hence:
Two roads diverged in a wood, and I—
I took the one less traveled by,
And that has made all the difference.

Syntax—the word order and how the phrases illuminate the poetry—almost like setting. If the words are in the wrong order, the intended effect by the poet will not be experienced. Correct word order will achieve the highest impact. That is why it is important, as mentioned earlier, to play around with words and stanzas until they achieve the desired emotion.

Theme—statement about the poem or the statement the poet is making about the subject.

Tone—the poet's attitude or expression of the subject which permeates throughout the poem. A subject is interpreted through a mood. When you have decided the mood, choose only the words that develop that emotion. A strong voice is what makes a poem exceptional.

TYPES OF POETRY

With more than fifty types of poetry, the following is a simple overview of the most well-known. Research and study many types of poetry to gain further understanding into some of the more complicated forms. Developing a true appreciation for all poetry forms will enable the poet to choose what the most appealing voice is for the poem.

FORMAL POETRY

A basic understanding of scansion is necessary for writing formal poetry. Scansion is "the action of scanning a line of verse to determine its rhythm; the rhythm of a line of verse."[19] In formal poetry, each line contains a set number of beats with a variety of stresses and accents—generally two or three syllables. Rhyming patterns are marked at the end of a sentence by a letter (A). If the second line does not rhyme with the first line, it takes a new letter (B), with new letters added with new rhymes. For example, if the first two lines rhyme and the second two lines rhyme, the pattern would be AABB. If the first and third lines do not rhyme with the other, but the second and fourth lines do, it would be ABCB. ABCB is a common rhyme scheme in poetry, especially in folk songs. Certain rules do apply in formal poetry so be sure to study the form before writing it. Learning rhyme schemes can be quite difficult, but once learned, they will not be forgotten.

---

19 *The Oxford Pocket Dictionary of Current English,* Oxford Press, 2007.

Ballad—used to tell stories and is often set to music. If the story is based on religious or political themes, it is called a hymn. Examples: *The Man From Snowy River* by A.B. (Banjo) Patterson and *The Walrus and the Carpenter* by Lewis Carroll.

Epic—a lengthy poem (can be the size of a book) or narrative poem that tells a story about the heroic achievements of the hero. Examples: Homer's *Iliad and Odyssey* and *Paradise Lost* by John Milton.

Sonnet—a beautiful form of poetry which has fourteen lines. William Shakespeare (1564–1616), English poet and playwright, is well-known for his formal poetry in sonnets, which essentially follow a set pattern in meter and rhyme. Sonnets are fourteen lines long and often have a set rhyme pattern of ABABABABCDECDE or can end with a separate two-line couplet (usually the lines are the same length and rhyme and form a complete thought). Many of Shakespeare's sonnets end with a couplet.

Depending on the language, the sonnet's rhyme schemes are different; they make use of short and long syllables of rhythm units. Shakespeare would add or delete syllables as needed (example: the word *against* became *'gainst*). In Elizabethan times, this was esteemed if it was done skillfully. Some of our modern words were formed by Shakespeare; for example, *specially* became *especially*. In the seventeenth century, developing new words was frowned upon in poetry. Techniques were becoming the tools of learning poetry, rather than developing language. As with any writing, poetry has changed as the years have passed.

William Shakespeare wrote 154 sonnets, and the following is one of his most beautiful.

Sonnet 116, Let Me Not to the Marriage of True Minds
William Shakespeare

Let me not to the marriage of true minds
Admit impediments. Love is not love
Which alters when it alteration finds,
Or bends with the remover to remove:
O no! It is an ever-fixed mark
That looks on tempests and is never shaken;
It is the star to every wandering bark,
Whose worth's unknown, although his height be taken.
Love's not Time's fool, though rosy lips and cheeks
Within his bending sickle's compass come:
Love alters not with his brief hours and weeks,
But bears it out even to the edge of doom.
If this be error and upon me proved,
I never writ, nor no man ever loved.

FREE VERSE

Writing free verse is like playing tennis with the net down.
~Robert Frost

Free verse is unrhymed with no set meter or structure, and the poet makes the rules. Compared to a song without rhyme, free verse usually has a lyrical quality. Free verse generally has some type of rhythm, and it may have repetition and sound, but it usually does not have a beat. Poets are free to decide where to break into stanzas of two or more lines. Thoughts can be broken into paragraphs or in mid-sentence. To some, it is the most difficult poetry to write because there is no set pattern until the poet creates one. However, free verse does have an underlying structure—tension and release, bursts and pauses. Some words have more power than others, so they should have a strong position in the poem. Lines should be broken to show an emotion, giving it more emphasis. Imagery should be bold and in patterns, giving definition to the words. By studying the techniques of free verse poets, and finding those you like, it will help with the development.

Walt Whitman (1819–1892), American poet, essayist, and journalist, is recognized as one of the first well-known poets of free verse. Free verse is considered the modern form of poetry, but it has been around for centuries, actually dating back as far as 1665 with Abraham Cowley. Free verse became the most popular form of poetry in the twentieth century with such poems as Walt Whitman's *Leaves of Grass*. Walt Whitman is known for breaking many of his poems into stanzas when the reader needed to take a breath. The following is a free verse, metaphorical (symbolic) poem written by Whitman. One of the greatest enjoyments of poetry is the interpretation: Is this poem referring to an actual city or the circle of friends? You decide.

I Dream'd in a Dream
by Walt Whitman

I dream'd in a dream I saw a city invincible to the attacks of the
whole of the rest of the earth,
I dream'd that was the new city of Friends,
Nothing was greater there than the quality of robust love,
it led the rest,
It was seen every hour in the actions of the men of that city,
And in all their looks and words.

POETRY TIPS

Find your voice—everyone is created to be different. You are unique and your writing should be as well. Make sure your voice is clear.

Do not copy famous poets. Study them, but seek to find your own unique expression. In journal writing, the words reflect what you feel. Begin there and see what comes from the emotions and words that you express in poetry.

Hook and last line—in all types of writing, including poetry, a powerful hook at the beginning must capture the reader's attention. The opening line should set the tone of the poem. That line should encourage readers to keep reading. Find a hook and build from there. Depending on the theme of the poem being written, it might need to have melodic, heartfelt, dynamic, or suspenseful words—perhaps zesty or gripping words. Pleasing sounds are memorable but predictable; add the unpredictable to add contrast.

The final words of the poem should leave a lasting memory. Try comparing the first and last lines. Use the same strong technique writing the first line as the last. Each should be equally compelling. Some poets use the same line for the first and last for effect. Do this only when it is strategic.

Do not generalize—write concrete and specific words. Readers need to follow where the poem leads—if the wording is too general, they will get lost. Be specific. Write from what you know and have experienced. Add vivid images.

Lines and Stanzas—check line lengths. Lines of different lengths may be needed to add layers of meaning. Short lines add punch. Long lines add emotional depth. Decide what best fits what you are writing. Stanzas (grouping of lines) should be used to pace the poem and create mood. Perhaps the longer stanzas should be broken up for more effect. Fragile, tender poetry may need to be in one stanza. Bottom line: Check to make sure each line and stanza is doing what it should.

Guide the reader—poetry should guide a reader to the theme—not push. Poetry grows as it progresses, pointing to the emotions and theme. The reader should experience the words along the way—not be pushed to an emotion that may or may not come.

Watch for clichés—if a saying has become overused, it loses its effectiveness. No creativity can shine through something old and used—senses are dulled and it shows laziness on the part of the poet. How many times have you heard these clichés? Blind as a bat, every cloud has a silver lining, busy as a bee, and easy as pie. If a cliché describes what you want to say, write it in a different way. Use a thesaurus to find words that enhance and guide.

Avoid overuse of adjectives and adverbs—too many adjectives and adverbs in poetry can bring an overabundance of imagery. Use strong nouns and verbs that give pictures and action, rather than trying to dress up words that are not clear in the beginning.

Rhyming—in formal poetry, rhyme and meter can easily sound like nursery rhymes with a child-like feeling. Poetry is not the easiest form of writing and overusing rhyme may cause loss of theme and depth.

Title—a title needs to be descriptive of the content and spark interest. Sometimes the first or last line of a poem works well for the title (if the repetition develops the content). If the title is suspenseful, make sure the content begins to quickly back up the title. Titles can convey more meaning, but make sure that meaning is clear and adds a layer to the poem.

Editing poetry—as with any writing, it is rare for the first draft to be the final draft in poetry. Rewrite until the poetry says all that you mean for it to say. Readers can get lost when too many images are given, so cut down the words if there are too many adjectives. Poetry needs to be precise. Every word should have meaning, so eliminate all the clutter. Nouns should give a picture when they are defined, and verbs should be active. Is each word essential to the poem's meaning? Does it bring the theme forward? Once changes have been made, let it sit for a few days, and then look at it again with fresh eyes. Does the poetry flow? Are the bursts and pauses helpful? Is the body of the poem understood? Look for verses that are hard to follow. What may have seemed so lyrical before may look confusing later. Perhaps stanzas will need to be moved to create a more logical order. Ask sincere friends to read your poem to see how they felt when they read it. Listen to any comments—good and bad. You may find the missing pieces and be able to take the poetry from good to amazing.

Poetry is a unique form of writing. It may be helpful to study books on poetry that give instruction on prosody (structure of poetry) and versification (writing verses). Books on poetic terms and how to learn the intricacies of the ballad, sonnet, and other forms should also be researched and studied as well. Writing poetry is a craft. If you have the opportunity, ask questions of those who have had their work published. Any tips will be helpful.

Every poet or songwriter has a voice. Whether it is in poetry or song, your voice should carry truth and conviction. Finding your unique voice is central to discovering the depth of your writing. C.S. Lewis gave the following advice to poets: "Look in thy heart and write . . . but when a poet looks in his heart he finds many things there besides the actual. That is why, and how, he is a poet."[20]

Martin Luther once said: "Music is the art of the prophets and a gift of God." The ability to write poetry and music is an art and gift from God. Find your passion, and your voice will rise up and be heard with words that will come straight from your heart.

I have never started a poem yet whose end I knew. Writing a poem is discovering.

~Robert Frost

20 Wayne Martindale and Jerry Root, *The Quotable Lewis,* Tyndale House Publishers, Wheaton, 1990, pg. 477, quoted from *English Literature in the Sixteenth Century,* pg. 328.

CHAPTER THIRTEEN

ESPECIALLY FOR WRITERS OF CHILDREN'S STORIES

Little Red Riding Hood was my first love. I felt that if I could have married Little Red Riding Hood I should have known perfect bliss.

~Charles Dickens
English novelist

Recently, I was renting a movie from a vending machine in a local grocery store. A line was forming behind me as we all waited for a boy who was about ten years old to rent his movies—not just one, but four, and they were all due back the next day. His whole day was going to be spent watching four movies. After the boy left, the man behind me said what I was thinking: "That kid needs to get a life!" How sad to think that watching movies was his entertainment for the day.

Movies, video games, television, and computers are luring kids away from the things many of us enjoyed as children, such as playing outside, playing with creative toys such as building blocks, and, most importantly, reading. If children do not develop a love for reading, they are going to miss out on one of the great joys of life and on the learning received from books. If we want kids to read, we are going to have to write something that they want to read. This is where you can make a difference.

CHILDREN NEED TO DREAM

Children's literature is a vast genre with a variety of choices for the children's writer to choose from. Fairy tales, legends, fables, tall tales, fantasy, historical fiction, contemporary fiction, classic rhymes, poetry, non-fiction biographies, scientific, and informational books are just some of the options to pursue.

Well-known children's writers before us laid a path to follow, but to be innovative, those paths must be extended to even greater lengths. Charles Perrault (1628–1703), French author who wrote *Cinderella, Little Red Riding Hood, Sleeping Beauty,* and *Puss in Boots,* is credited with writing the first fairy tales. He laid a clear path for future children's fairy tale writers such as The Brothers Grimm (Jacob, 1785–1863 and Wilhelm, 1786–1859) and Hans Christian Anderson (1805–1875). These and many others have written classic books for children that will be treasured by generations to come. Perhaps the book that you write will be listed as one of the great children's stories of all time.

Creative non-fiction is becoming a new genre in children's and adult's writing. This genre combines the elements of both fiction and non-fiction, giving the best of both. The market for non-fiction books for children is growing, so it is an excellent genre in which to write. Writing non-fiction is educational—not only to the children reading the book, but to the writer as well. Writers who research will find creative, unusual and enthusiastic angles. As a result, freshness will flow in the writing, making it all the more enjoyable and educational for the reader.

READ

The stories of childhood leave an indelible impression, and their author always has a niche in the temple of memory from which the image is never cast out....

~Howard Pyle
American illustrator

What we read as children usually stays with us most of our lives. Favorite books that became tattered and dog-eared from reading them so many times are masterpieces because of the countless hours of enjoyment that came from them. That is the type of book every children's story writer hopes to create—something that could forever be special in the heart of a child.

Reading books as children enhances imagination, giving the inspiration to achieve. Funny and adventurous stories, fantasies, and fairy tales, where anything can happen, are within reach in the pages of a book. Through imaginatively written books, children are being educated, though they may not even realize it. Hopes and dreams can begin to form into aspirations of future careers, such as being an athlete, dancer, singer, doctor, author, and so much more.

Do you remember your favorite books as a child? Read those again. Think about why you enjoyed those books. Read classics in children's literature. They are classics for a reason—they are ageless and fresh, generation after generation. Study them, and then read books that have recently been published which are bestsellers. Notice changes. Read books that are in the age group and genre that you wish to write. Learn what you can from the writings of others, but remember you are unique; so your work should be original and creative. Dr. Seuss, a master with children's rhymes, said: "Today you are you, that is truer than true! There is no one alive who is youer than you!"

WRITE ON THEIR LEVEL

A kid is a guy I never wrote down to. He's interested in what I say if I make it interesting.

~Theodore Geisel (Dr. Seuss)

When writing children's books, it is important *not* to write from a babyish place, but rather a childlike place. Children's stories should have the same engaging elements as adult fiction but on a level that children can relate to and understand. When deciding what and how to write for children, understanding age appropriateness is important because children act, think, and speak differently at various ages. Once the age group is determined and the concept for the story is set, the writing can begin.

Many children's writers want to include animals that talk in their children's stories, which can be creative or a complete blunder. Bunnies that are cute and cuddly might be acceptable for a baby board book, but unacceptable for a chapter book. Use the name *rabbit*, not bunny, for older children. If animals are going to be written in a fictional story, they need to be developed just as human characters would be developed. Personalities, mannerisms, and other characteristics should make the animal unique. Is the rabbit sly and smart, but he blinks when he is nervous? Study animals to discover how they move and sound. Add those observations to human characteristics to make them seem real. Research behaviors and all that you can about an animal if you are going to attempt to write about one.

In *C.S. Lewis, Letters to Children,* Lewis was asked to give comments regarding some stories about animals a little girl named Joan had sent to him. He said,

> *The main fault of the animal one is that you don't mix the reality and the fantasy quite in the right way. One way is Beatrix Potter's or Brer Rabbit's. By fantasy the animals are allowed to talk and behave*

in many ways like humans. But their relations to one another and to us remain the real ones. Rabbits are in danger from foxes and men. The other way is mine: You go right out of this world into a different creation, where there are different sorts of animals. Yours are all in the real world with a real eclipse. But they don't have the real relations to one another—small animals would not be friends with an owl, nor would it know more astronomy than they . . . I hope you don't mind me telling you all this? One can learn only by seeing one's mistakes.[21]

SPEND TIME WITH CHILDREN

Some children (evacuees) stayed with C.S. Lewis during World War II. When he observed their behavior, the thought occurred to him to write a story for them because they always seemed to want something to do (the same as children today). Thus he began writing his amazing series *The Chronicles of Narnia*. I recently read his seven-book series again, and I enjoyed them just as much, if not more, as I did when I was a child. C.S. Lewis said, "A book worth reading only in childhood is not worth reading even then." He felt children's stories should be enjoyable to everyone at all ages. Something almost magical is imparted as we step into the place where fairy tales and dreams come true in stories. Adults need that too.

Children are constantly experiencing new things because they are discovering the world they live in—vitality and life are expressed. Children view life differently than adults. For example, if a child was given a toy truck, he would probably go outside, make some paths for the truck to drive on, drive speedily down those paths, pick up friends along the way (though they may be stones, they are his friends), and then stop at a lake to swim (a puddle). If an adult was given a toy truck, he would look at how it was made. Is it sturdy? Is it plastic or steel? Do the wheels turn correctly? You get the picture.

21 Lyle W. Dorsett and Marjorie Lamp Mead, *C.S. Lewis, Letters to Children,* Touchstone, New York, 1985, pg 80.

To write for children, the author needs to understand how children think. Try to remember how you might relate to a situation as a child. If you can find that place, remarkable stories can be written. Spend time and listen to children—how they talk and reason. When children do not think anyone is watching, they will be freer to become who they have imagined. Their current world transforms to wherever their imaginations will take them. Listen to their dialogue and the sounds they make. See how they solve problems and watch how an adventure unfolds. Children know how to describe in simple but wonderful ways, so take notes and review any patterns you see. The fun you will see children experience is a sample of what they might like in a book. Inspirational ideas for children's books can come at any time or any place. Look for ideas in everyday life. Humorous and meaningful situations happen all the time, so keep a writing journal with you to note them.

CHILDHOOD MEMORIES

All of us have had life-changing experiences. When a life-changing experience happens, especially as children, it will affect us for the rest of our lives. What we have experienced or seen others experience can become life in our stories.

When I was ten years old, I visited the National Zoo in Washington, D.C. I love animals, and spending a whole day looking at hundreds of them is one of my favorite childhood memories. The gray wolves were by far my favorite. I remember clearly the focused look of a particular wolf—I was in awe of his beautiful and unwavering gaze. I thought he must be the leader of the pack because of his large size. The more I watched him, the more I wanted him to be free—to live with his kind in a pack of wolves. The picture of that wolf has remained etched in my memory to this day. When I began writing my fictional work, *The Chosen Path*, there was no question that wolves were going to play a big part in the story. When I wrote about Brogan, Zoe's wolf, he came to life from my memory of that wolf in the zoo. Brogan lived the kind of life I wanted that wolf to live.

Writing from a place of experience brings life to writing. To jog childhood memories, it is helpful to make a trip to places where you may have played or visited as a child, such as the following: playgrounds, swimming pools, the beach, mountains, children's movies, parks, zoos, restaurants, anywhere you vacationed as a child, and so on. You will be surprised by what you will remember when you revisit a favorite place. What are some of your favorite childhood memories? Try to remember how you felt—your emotions. Write down what you can recall in your writer's journal. Do you remember the first time you experienced something new in your life? Write every detail. Think about your first roller coaster ride. What did it feel like? If you had any pets, think about your first one. Special memories are associated with that pet. Now think about an adventure that could happen with that pet. Write anything down that comes to mind and save for future use.

Recently, I visited a friend's art show. Of the many beautiful photographs that were in the exhibit, I was drawn to a photograph of a brown, orange, red, and yellow spotted wooden horse that was on a carousel. I thought at first it was the bright colors that drew me to the picture, but then I realized, that was not why I loved that picture. When I was young, we visited Pullen Park in Raleigh, North Carolina, where there was an old-fashioned carousel with all kinds of antique wooden animals that children could ride. That picture jogged pleasant memories of the many hours spent at that park. It reminded me also of a train that wound around the park's circumference. Many hours were spent riding that train with my own children. That picture brought those fond memories back to me vividly. I purchased the carousel horse photograph, and now I can gaze at it and remember those pleasant days at Pullen Park. While I am writing this paragraph, I am thinking about a number of adventures that could be written just from that memory. Memorable experiences as children stay with us our whole lives, and they are a powerful tool in writing.

Every day something new is experienced that later can be written in a story. If something memorable happens, be sure to write it down right then. Personal situations and names can be changed to fit a setting. The story can be enhanced by adding new adventures and characters. Consider how memories can be a convincing part of any story. The more real something is to you, the more real it will be to those who read your book. Writing goes to a new level when it is written from experience.

EMOTIONS

Children have extreme emotions. When children see something for the first time, their senses are alerted to experience all that they can. Nothing is held back in experiencing that moment. They know how to display sheer abandon when they are excited. When they are hurt, everyone in the house will hear them crying. When they are happy, they might jump up and down and laugh until it is contagious. By observing children and their emotions, it will help children's authors to write real-life emotions of children in a book.

Practice writing emotions so they become life-like. Try not to use exclamation points; use words that express. Try to write using the five senses—hearing, seeing, touching, smelling, and tasting. Search until you find a word that communicates the feeling.

HUMOR

I like nonsense, it wakes up the brain cells. Fantasy is a necessary ingredient in living, it's a way of looking at life through the wrong end of a telescope, which is what I do, and that enables you to laugh at life's realities.

~Theodore Geisel (Dr. Seuss)

Children love to laugh. Humor in children's stories is a definite plus because it will keep children reading. If a parent is reading the book to his or her child, it is all the more fun when both are able to laugh at the same scene. For forty-five years, Dr. Seuss was a master at writing made-up, silly words. Children love the types of words and humor found in his stories. Dr. Seuss describes his alphabet like this: "My alphabet starts with this letter called yuzz. It's the letter I use to spell yuzz-a-ma-tuzz. You'll be sort of surprised what there is to be found once you go beyond 'Z' and start poking around!"

If you want to know what makes children laugh, watch television with them and see what makes them giggle. Take notes in your writing journal about what they laugh about in certain situations and characters because it may help you to see a pattern about what is funny to them.

With young children, the humor must be progressive so that they are following the joke; then the punch line can be given. A play on words is fun within an absurd scene. Tongue-twisting names and silly pronunciations make children laugh. Children love the ridiculous.

Charles Schulz was a genius with humor. He could make all ages laugh with the exaggeration in his characters of Charlie Brown, Linus, Snoopy, Lucy, and many others in the *Peanuts* cartoon. The scene at the Peanuts gang's Christmas play is my all-time favorite. Lucy is auditioning Snoopy for all the animal parts in the play, and of course, he is magnificent at playing every animal he auditions for. She asks, "How about a penguin?" Snoopy, with his feet turned out, waddles around her just like a penguin. Lucy shouts, "Yes, he's even a good penguin." Snoopy suddenly jumps on her head, and Lucy screams, "No! No! No!" He falls flat on his back while Lucy continues her tirade. Next he jumps up and stands beside her, mimicking everything she does. Out of Lucy's frustration, she lectures those in the play, "Listen all of you! You've got to take direction! You've got to have discipline!

You've got to have respect for your director!" Slyly, Lucy turns to see what Snoopy is doing. She pulls up her fist, "I oughtta slug you!" Snoopy with all his dog charm gives her a big, wet kiss, and she runs in circles, screaming, "Ugh!!! I've been kissed by a dog! I have dog germs. Get some hot water! Get some disinfectant! Get some Iodine!" And we all laugh at the absurdity of the whole scene.

When I taught second grade, one year the children in my class discovered that I loved Warheads, an extremely sour candy. Almost every morning someone would bring me a piece of that candy just to see my face. Every time I ate one, my eyes would squint as tears formed and my face would turn red as I grimaced with the sourness of that candy. The children would laugh every time. It was just a simple thing, but to them it was hilarious. Children laugh at the ridiculous. They really do understand far more than many adults give them credit for. That is why it is so important to understand how children react at different ages—then you will know how to write for that age group.

Sometimes when I get up in the morning, I feel very peculiar. I feel like I've just got to bite a cat! I feel like if I don't bite a cat before sundown, I'll go crazy! But then I just take a deep breath and forget about it. That's what is known as real maturity.

~Quote from Snoopy in *Peanuts* by Charles Schulz

FIRST OR THIRD PERSON

Novels written in first person are popular with middle grade and young adult readers. The story is told by one of the characters, and it is instantly relatable if written well. Written from the "I" point of view, first person stories need to be witty and full of emotion. However, first person is not recommended for younger readers because it can confuse them. Why? Limitations occur because the child can only know what the main character feels and sees, so he or she has the task of deciding what really happens. Most young children are not yet ready to do this.

Third person point of view is well-liked by most any age because the narrator can give more observations and use more sophisticated language. Whether the book is written in first or third person, the story's point of view should be seen through the eyes of the main characters. The narrator should only tell what the characters know—it will be confusing otherwise. Avoid long narration and description in a child's book. See Chapter Ten, "Especially for Fiction Writers" for more information on point of view.

STORYLINE

"Begin at the beginning," the King said, very gravely, "and go on till you come to the end: then stop."
~Quote from *Alice in Wonderland,* written by Lewis Carroll

All stories should have a beginning, middle, and ending. Action should start at the beginning to draw interest. Something should happen that brings the main character into some conflict in the beginning, then it is dealt with in the middle, and it is resolved at the end. The story should come to a prompt ending. Most important to remember: Children's stories must have a happy ending.

Note cards are helpful to organize a story because different parts can be moved around so the most logical order can be determined. Separate the main parts of the story, and then write them on the note cards. You can fill in the secondary parts later.

SETTING

Details about the setting are of little interest to children, unless there is action associated with it. The setting needs to play a part in the action—an interesting place or something familiar. For example, if the story's setting is at a crystal clear blue lake on a hot day, include that setting into an action scene. The following is the beginning of a little story that I wrote just for this book with the setting at a lake to give you an example of using the setting with action and intrigue to catch a child's attention at the beginning.

Jeremy was sure of it. Something had just moved in the lake. There—he saw it again. As the water rippled, a dolphin-sized orange fish jumped out of the water and back in. In that split moment, he had looked Jeremy right in the eyes. That was no ordinary fish.

Down the river, Jeremy saw a fisherman paddling his boat in the water. He wanted to tell him about the fish, but thought better of the idea. Somehow it just didn't seem right for that fisherman or anyone to catch that fish. He didn't know why he felt that way. He just did.

Jeremy watched from shore as the fisherman hurried to get his line in the water. With lightning speed, that same orange fish jumped into the fisherman's boat, knocked his bait and pole into the water, slapped him in the face with his fin, and jumped back in the water. He could hear that fisherman yelling all the way to the shore, "I'm gonna get you if it's the last thing I do!"

All Jeremy could do was laugh. He was glad the old fisherman didn't catch that fish. Little did Jeremy know that soon, he would have his own meeting with the fish, and that his life would never be the same.

The above is an example of the first chapter in a story geared for children ages 7–10. A story for this age group needs to gallop before them, inviting them to want to turn the pages. A hook should be left at the end of each chapter to encourage the child to keep reading. Chapters should build until finally the climax brings the story to closure. As the story progresses, more dialogue should be written. Use age-appropriate dialogue and actions for characters. Write scenes so that the reader will know who said what and how, without the word *said* which can be easily overused. Avoid using the words *exclaimed* and *shouted*. There will be no need to use the word *exclaim* if the actions in the scene are written well. In dialogue, use direct quotes instead of indirect quotes. For example, write "Get back!" instead of "She told him to stand back."

CHARACTERS AND PLOT

A dynamic plot and characters should match. Most children's books are character-driven plots. Conflict should grow in intensity so it will hold the child's attention. Events in the story move the plot forward. The main character needs to resolve the conflict, not an adult or outsider. It should be a child-like solution—not as an adult would solve the problem.

The main characters are either humans, fantasy creatures, or animals. Characters need to be likeable—kids need to be able to relate to and sympathize with them. Be assured—if a child does not like the main character, he or she will not read the book. Characters need to be identified with simple physical traits, some quirky or interesting mannerism, and perhaps a favorite phrase. Characters should be written so that children want to emulate them—brave, strong, and with true respect for those they associate with.

Characters need to evolve; they should fail and succeed for the plot to be realistic. The character needs to grow in the process. Give children hope that heroes and heroines will rise up and conquer. We all make mistakes in life, so when a character does something wrong, write the story so that the character rises and makes things right once again. The character should overcome something to succeed.

Characters should not have long names or names that begin with the same letter. Children will become confused and it will make the story harder to follow. A name should be memorable and fitting to the character.

Evil should be evil and good should be good, not mixed so children are confused. With adventure, there is always a villain—make him a villain so that children can understand the differences between right and wrong.

Respect and honor for those older is not what it once was in movies, television shows, and books. All too often, children speak disrespectfully to parents and authority figures in their lives. Children learn from what they see and hear. Write so authority figures such as parents, teachers, and friends are given respect so that children understand to honor them.

PLOT SEQUENCE

1. Conflict
2. Tension—character is attempting to solve the conflict
3. Possible failure
4. Victory
5. Outcome of victory

PICTURES IN BOOKS

Books geared for children up to six years old should always have illustrations. Jon Amos Comenius (1592–1670), a Czech writer, innovative thinker, educator, teacher, and scientist, who is considered the father of modern education, wrote *Orbis Pictus,* which is thought to be the first picture book specifically for children.

Examples of some of the most popular picture books include the following: Eric Carle's *The Hungry Caterpillar,* Beatrix Potter's *The Tale of Peter Rabbit,* Maurice Sendak's *Where the Wild Things Are,* Dr. Seuss' *Green Eggs and Ham,* and Robert McCloskey's *Make Way for Ducklings.* These authors also illustrated the pictures in their books.

Note: If you are an illustrator, draw the pictures and submit them to a publisher with the story. If you are *not* an illustrator, do not submit drawings with the story. Be open to another illustrator working on your book, which should be stated in a cover letter with the submission of your manuscript. Editors know a good story when they read one, so if the story is approved for publishing, a professional artist will be hired to draw the pictures. Writers generally do not have any input with the illustrations unless it is agreed upon in the contract. Sometimes meaningful suggestions may be allowed, but the publisher will have the last word on approval of the pictures. Professional illustrators have good conceptual ideas, and they will draw to match the storyline.

DIFFERENT TYPES OF CHILDREN'S BOOKS

Obviously, children's books should not be the length of adult books because children's attention spans are shorter. As children grow older, the length and the vocabulary in the book will increase, and the amount of pictures will decrease. Memorable children's books have strong themes—whether fiction or non-fiction. Age groups for children's literature are sometimes difficult to define because different ages will read among the various types of books. The following are general guidelines to help you to decide which age group you would like to write for. Become acquainted with the market—every publishing house is different. If you are interested in certain publishers printing your book, contact them about the type of books they want to publish at the time, including word count, formatting, and other questions you might have.

BABY BOARD BOOK

The earliest and simplest type of children's book is meant to take wear and tear from babies who are teething. Board books are made of thick cardboard or plastic. Generally, they are about twelve pages. The simplest baby board books have no words, and as they graduate, some will have just a few words and simple pictures on each page. Many parents like these books for babies who are just learning to talk because of the word association with a picture. Board books have word counts that vary from approximately 20–100 words. *Goodnight Moon* by Margaret Wise Brown is a classic, popular bedtime board book.

NOVELTY BOOK

Toddlers usually love these colorful, simple books with "things" to do on each page—from feeling a fluffy bunny tail to opening doors to see what is behind them. *Pat the Bunny*, by Dorothy Kunhardt, is a popular novelty book, which was written for the author's three-year-old daughter. With the language of a toddler expanding, the child learns by touching. Novelty books are made with similar materials as board books. Word counts are typically more than a board book because there is a short storyline. Word counts are typically 100–200 words.

PICTURE BOOK

The best picture books are warm and humorous and are meant to be read over and over. *The Pokey Little Puppy* (Golden Books, 1942), by Janette Sebring Lowrey, is still the best-selling hardcover children's picture book of all time. The storyline and illustrations are simple, but the sentences are longer in a picture book. Picture books graduate from simple to more difficult storylines, and pictures decrease as the word count and page numbers increase.

When writing a picture book, it is best to think with pictures and the text. Make a chart and block off the amount of pages to be used. Use note cards to write the text per page. Move the note cards around so that the sequence is logical. It should be exciting—each page should make the child want to turn the page and read what is next. Each page should have an illustration that can be easily drawn from the text. There should be no more than two or three characters. Picture books vary in page count due to the way they are cut and bound. Format constrictions do apply, so it is best to consult a publishing house to understand their restrictions. The paper in picture books is usually durable and heavy for rough-handling. Children will need to have the ability to turn pages to enjoy a picture book, but they also enjoy others reading it to them. The following are average word counts. Note: Non-fiction children's books are typically longer than fiction.

Preschool picture book (ages 1–3): 20–300 words (depending on age)

Early picture book (ages 4–8): less than 1,000 words

Traditional picture book: less than 1,200 words

Non-fiction picture books: up to 2,000 words. Note: Biographies written for children are in great demand because there are not enough of them.

EASY READERS

Written for early elementary grades (ages 6–8), these books still have color illustrations (usually on every page) and a simple storyline in both fiction and non-fiction. The story is sometimes separated into short chapters. Longer words are used with action, and dialogue is a big part. Children can now read independently, but some children in this age group are still learning to follow print from right to left. A child who is beginning to read independently will still enjoy listening to difficult and exciting books that are written for older kids. Still, they want that kind of story in books they can read. The easy reader writer needs to develop a storyline that is still exciting and has depth but is also something a child can master in reading.

Easy readers have four levels which typically signify grade levels. Each chapter consists of several pages. The lower the level, the larger the typeset with fewer and simpler words. Each level progresses in the number of words per page. Word counts vary greatly by the publisher, so be sure to contact individual publishers for guidelines. A beginner easy reader begins with five to seven words per line, and most are sight words (words that are easily recognizable). The word count for beginner easy readers begins around 200 words, but by level four, they progress to around 1,500 words (32–64 pages of text). *Amelia Bedelia* by Peggy Parrish and *Little Bear* by Else Holmelund Minarik are classic examples of popular easy readers.

EARLY CHAPTER BOOKS (ALSO CALLED TRANSITION BOOKS)

Early chapter books are written for ages 7–10. The transition from picture books to chapter books is a special time for a child because the books are more "grown-up." Fewer illustrations are in early chapter books—children can now picture the plot in their minds. The words are still somewhat simple for this age group, so children's writers have a challenge to write enthralling books that help them grow in their enjoyment of reading. *Stepping Stone Books* by Random House are popular early chapter books. *Frog and Toad* books by Arnold Lobel and *Ramona* books by Beverly Cleary are classic examples of easy chapter books. These books are typically 48–64 pages with word counts that range from 500–3,000. Sentences are more thought-provoking and longer, but paragraphs are still short (2–4 sentences).

MIDDLE GRADE CHAPTER BOOKS

Kids begin to truly enjoy reading at this level. These books are typically written for middle grades (Grades 4-7, ages 10–12). Children at this age are good readers because their vocabulary has increased. Fewer illustrations are in middle grade books, and if there are any, they are typically black and white. The chapters suddenly become longer and the words more difficult. The typeset and size of the book is smaller.

Characters need to change and grow, but it is more of an inward change. Some type of conflict must occur with the main character to make him or her grow. Dialogue and characters need to be believable—kids will be quick to detect a book that is "cheesy" (stupid or tacky). Secondary characters can be added at this level. The topics are broader than beginner chapter books—friendships, school situations, relationships with siblings, and how to live and operate within their environment are appropriate topics. Puberty is beginning and they are trying to find their identities. Be sure to add an end-of-the-chapter hook to keep this age group interested in finishing the book.

Average word counts range from 10,000–40,000. Middle grade books have a huge market because they are sold through book clubs and elementary book fairs at schools, where kids choose their books rather than parents. One of the fictional bestsellers in paperback is *Charlotte's Web* by E.B. White, and one of the best-known classic middle grade chapter books is *A Wrinkle in Time* by Madeleine L'Engle.

YOUNG ADULT BOOKS

Typically, young adult books are written for ages twelve and up. However, a new category is emerging for kids ages 10–14, especially in the young adult fiction genre. Spend some time with kids this age and study books on how adolescents progress in thinking and reacting—this will greatly help in determining how to write for them.

Mark Twain's classic book, *Adventures of Huckleberry Finn,* was originally written for adults, but young adults enjoy this book as well. While it is important for writers to have a target audience when writing for children, different age groups will read it. Some kids with exceptional reading abilities have already transitioned to adult novels, but some material is definitely not appropriate for them.

Many adolescents have been exposed to adult themes through movies, television, and books, so they are aware of how the adult world is projected through that medium. Writers for young adults will need to capture their attention with material they are interested in, but will need to steer away from adult problems and issues. Books need to be geared to teens, their problems, hopes, and the issues that affect them. They are becoming concerned about the environment, good vs. evil, justice, and social issues. Their minds are open, and it is a great opportunity for those who have a passion for this age group to write inspirational and thought-provoking fiction and non-fiction works. They are searching and they will find something. Why not bring them hope—that they can make a difference in this world?

Novels for young adults need to become more sophisticated. Several main characters should be added with a more complex plot and subplots. An adolescent is typically the protagonist with the application of age-appropriate storylines and subjects. Adventures with unusual and creative plots that are intriguing will get attention from this age group. The writing field is open for young adult books—fantasy, mystery, romance, contemporary Christian fiction, e-books, and most any genre that is written for adults. The stipulation is that it needs to be age-appropriate. Classics for this age group include such books such as *The Swiss Family Robinson* (1812) by Johann David Wyss, which was one of the earliest novels written for young adults. Other fine classic examples are the following: *Little Women* (1868) by Louisa May Alcott, *Anne of Green Gables* (1908) by Lucy Maud Montgomery, and *The Chronicles of Narnia* series by C.S. Lewis (1950-1956). In the young adult book, word counts range from 40,000–60,000 words.

EDITING YOUR WRITING

When you finally finish your manuscript, be sure to check for grammar and spelling. Read Chapter Nine in this book on "The Skill of Editing" for detailed instruction. Proper editing can make the difference between rejection or acceptance of your manuscript by a publisher.

Ask age-appropriate children to read your manuscript. Listen to their thoughts. Children can be brutally honest, which is exactly what you will need to hear. After they have read your manuscript, ask them the following questions:

1) Did you like the book? Why?

2) What did you like most in the book?

3) What did you like least?

4) Who was your favorite character?

5) Were there any characters you didn't like? Why?

6) Is there anything you would change?

7) Is there anything you would have liked to happen in the story?

8) Did the story end like you wanted it to?

9) How did it make you feel?

10) Would you like to read more books with the same characters?

Write down all the answers in detail. If the answers are consistently the same to the questions, you should rewrite those parts. Kids know what they like.

While researching material for this section, I discovered that many who have written for children say it is the work they are most proud of. Some of these authors have written adult fiction stories and said there was no comparison in the fulfillment they experienced in writing for children. Writing for children is a noble career; after all, what they learn as children will shape them into who they become as adults. If you love children and writing, write for them. That love will be like a thread sown in and out of your writing, which is what all children need to experience.

Dark stories pervade the market, and too much darkness is on television. Surely, as children's writers, books that have thrilling adventures can be written without darkness saturating them. Since 9/11, now more than ever, many publishing companies have been looking for "feel good" stories. Children need to be children—laughing and enjoying life. All too soon adulthood will be upon them with all the responsibilities that go with it. Think about what you want to leave as a legacy in writing—a book that brings sadness to a child or one that brings hope and joy? What you write is a legacy, and that is an amazing thought. You have the opportunity to help a child grow in character and aspirations in life. Choice words make the adventure come to life and leave memories to be treasured always.

I am almost included to set it up as a canon that a children's story which is enjoyed only by children is a bad children's story. The good ones last. A waltz which you can like only when you are waltzing is a bad waltz.[22]

~C.S. Lewis

22 Wayne Martindale and Jerry Root, *The Quotable Lewis,* Tyndale House Publishers, Wheaton, 1990, pg. 90, quoted from *Of Other Worlds: Essays and Stories,* "On Three Ways of Writing for Children", pg. 24.

CHAPTER FOURTEEN

ESPECIALLY FOR INSPIRATIONAL WRITERS

Aim at heaven and you will get earth thrown in. Aim at earth and you get neither.

~C. S. Lewis

The world today wants electrifying action, but often with it comes darkness that permeates the plots in movies, television programs, and books. Inspirational writers have the opportunity to write in all types of genres from a place of light, giving solid foundational truths with the action.

Christians should be writing the most inspirational and light-filled books in the world because of knowing the truest Inspiration of all—the Lord. The brighter the light within us, the more passionate and inspirational our words will be. Flowing from our pens should be the most creative, cutting-edge writing.

Genesis 2:7 tells us, **"Then the LORD God formed man of dust from the ground, and breathed into his nostrils the breath of life; and man became a living being."** We see here that God breathed into man's nostrils and then man received breath—the breath of God. Wherever God breathes, life is brought forth. Every breath taken is the breath of God. His life is within us—His inspiration is flowing through us. Since inspiration is already within, the key is to discover creativity and use it. All have His *breath* flowing through them, but those who know Him have the added advantage of His *light* within them.

WRITING WITH HOPE

There is quite enough sorrow and shame and suffering and baseness in real life, and there is no need for meeting it unnecessarily in fiction.

~Theodore Roosevelt

I once wrote a non-fiction inspirational article in which I was quite adamant about the subject. I gave it to a friend to read and he said, "You know, people can swallow sugar better than vinegar." When I reread the article, I realized that I had written it almost in a condemning way—like I was trying to ram my beliefs into my writing so readers could grasp what I was trying to say. From my friend's statement and rewriting that article, I learned something that has helped me in all my future writing. No matter how strongly I believe in something, I cannot force it onto someone. I rewrote the article, but I wrote it from the foundation of love with a thread of hope sown throughout. The article was published.

When an article or book is written too harshly, the arrow goes right past the target and lands on the ground. An arrow will hit the target when it is written in a firm but gentle and strategic way. Unless we have walked in the shoes of others, we do not know what has brought them to a particular place in their lives. That is why it is important to not talk down to or judge people in writing. Avoid being preachy or lecturing. Condemnation will not bring anyone to the light. When people feel condemned by others, guilt or rebellion will be the result, and many times they will turn away from the truth and their friends and family, the very ones who could possibly help them.

Respect your readers. Be compassionate and sensitive, and pray for wisdom and guidance when writing. People who want to put their pasts behind them are looking for hope. They need the reassurance that God has not abandoned them and that He still loves them. Psalm 46:1 tell us this: **"God is our refuge and strength, always ready to help in times of trouble"** (NLT). People need to know that.

Experiences bring life to writing. When those experiences are expressed with honesty and encouragement, they will bring hope to readers. Stay true to who you are in writing. Truth comes from what has become real to you—your perceptions. You can only write with passion what has become life within you. If the Lord has been helping you in a certain area and you have had success in overcoming it, new life will be bursting forth from you to tell others and to write about what you have learned. Write while you are inspired like this—writing with passion will change lives. For example, in your past you may have had anger issues. Write about those issues and how you took steps to overcome them. Those with the same issues might relate and find the very help they have been searching for through what you have written. Readers will see that since you overcame, perhaps there is hope for them. Be sure to include Scriptures to reinforce what you are saying.

In inspirational fiction, characters need to face trials because that is reality in life, but they should rise again, launching the message of overcoming. In some novels, it is hard to distinguish the good guys from the bad guys. A good character should emulate good, and an evil character should emulate evil. Heroes and heroines should overcome, have courage, and display strength.

C.S. Lewis did not begin writing *The Chronicles of Narnia* with the awareness of Christianity in the book. Lewis said this about his series: "Some people seem to think I began by asking myself how I could say something about Christianity to children . . . I couldn't write in that way at all. Everything began with images, a faun with an umbrella, a queen on a sledge, a magnificent lion. At first there wasn't even anything Christian about them; that element pushed in of its own accord."[23] I believe his books had Christian elements throughout them because being a Christian was so much of who C.S. Lewis was—he wrote from the place of enlightenment because he was enlightened. Lewis once said: "I believe in Christianity as I believe that the sun has risen: not only because I see it, but because by it I see everything else." Christian values could not help but come forth in his writing.

FRIENDS OF GOD

Friends share the closest, personal thoughts. I have always felt that this is what God wants with us—to be His friend. He will then begin to share amazing revelation—special things from His heart. I believe the Lord inspires us to write what He wants written. It is as simple as that. We just have to be willing to listen to His voice. Words from the heart of God will change lives. Be sure to write all that the Lord gives you in a journal so it will be ready to use when needed.

USE YOUR GIFT

The best-known Christian evangelist of the twentieth century is Billy Graham. He gained world attention in 1949 with a tent revival in downtown Los Angeles that was scheduled for three weeks but ended up lasting six. In the next fifty-five years and more, "Billy Graham Crusades" consistently drew audiences of thousands to

23 Lyle W. Dorsett and Marjorie Lamp Mead, *C.S. Lewis, Letters to Children,* Touchstone, New York, 1985, pg. 6

arenas and stadiums throughout the world. Millions have been saved through his ministry. He had an amazing gift and he used it. That is the point—he used it.

What good is any gift if it just sits on the shelf, waiting to be used at a convenient time? The gift of writing must be used for the gift to grow. Writing is difficult, but I can honestly say from experience that the more I write, the easier it becomes.

Many passionate writers from the past and present have writings that will last forever. C.S. Lewis was just such a writer. By now I am sure you know that he is one of my favorite authors from the many examples and quotes I have used from him in this book. Although he died in 1963, his thirty books live on, and he is still one of the most popular Christian authors today. Lewis was an atheist when he first began writing, but when he became a Christian, he also became powerfully passionate about his beliefs. It was only after he came to know Jesus that his writing was ignited to new levels. He had an incredible way of writing about the gospel so that anyone could understand. He had a unique talent of getting directly to the point and could write in any category. C.S. Lewis had a rare talent, and he used what he had so it grew. The same will be true for the inspirational writer.

WHEN WRITING BEGINS

The first time anything is accomplished, it brings amazing joy. I remember the first time I was able to play chords fast enough on my guitar so that they actually sounded somewhat like a song. I will never forget that joy of accomplishment. It is the same with writing. Writing is hard in the beginning, but when it is finally completed, the joy of accomplishment makes it well worth the struggle.

It took me seven years to finally finish my first novel, *The Chosen Path*. I had no real writing experience other than what I wrote in college. I felt I did not have the talent to write, but I kept persevering and wrote almost daily. During my sixth year of writing the book, everything started coming together. I began to see parts of the book like a movie. The book began to take life—I could feel it. I studied people and read more books about putting life into fiction. I asked the Lord to help me write what needed to be said. My brother, Rick Joyner, an accomplished writer, also helped me tremendously with the book (he was my editor). I became excited all over again, and I went back and rewrote scenes with added life. I felt a new depth of emotions in the characters. New creativity began to flow that I never had before. I actually had a great deal of fun with the scenes as I explored new ways of writing. After seven years of writing *The Chosen Path*, it was approved to be published. Can you imagine my joy? It will be the same for you. Keep persevering, and you will finish that writing project.

Some writing projects take longer than others. If you will submit to what the Lord is doing in you while you are writing, not only will you write your best work, you will write what you have learned which gives life to anything written. Part of the delay in finishing *The Chosen Path* was that the Lord was actually dealing with some of the same areas in my life that were happening to Zoe, the main character in the book. I could not write some parts of the book until that truth was real to me. So submit to the Lord's work in you and see new life come forth in your writing. Just do not quit.

USING THE BIBLE IN INSPIRATIONAL WRITING

In writing, we need to be able to back up what we are saying with research. In inspirational writing, Bible references are the catalyst in substantiating points. I enjoy using the *Biblesoft* computer program that has a *Strong's Concordance*, commentaries, Scripture references, dictionary, and a Bible encyclopedia. By using the quick tools on this program, it is easy to find a reference and then copy and paste it into the manuscript. Why is the Bible so important in inspirational writing? Let's see why.

II Timothy 3:16 tells us that: **"All Scripture is inspired by God and profitable for teaching, for reproof, for correction, for training in righteousness."** The Greek translation for **"inspired by God"** is "divinely breathed in," so from this we can see that *God breathed on His Words.* Breath represents life. The Bible contains God's life—His inspired Words. By using Bible references in writing, it will bring life to words.

If you want to write powerful books and articles, do two things: 1) Spend time with the Lord, who is the Word, and 2) read His Word, the Bible. It sounds simple and it is. Inspiration comes from spending time with the One who is true Inspiration. Reading His Word will bring new life into your life, which is when you will receive life-changing words to share with others. God's Words are powerful. By reading His Words, that power is being given to us and will ignite creativity and passion within to write life-changing books. Not only will you find the greatest subject matter to testify on any non-fiction topic such as courage, maintaining peace in life, overcoming depression, and thousands more, but you will find remarkable ideas for fictional works as well.

The Bible has many different themes in writing. The following are just some of them: humor, romance, betrayal, intrigue, revenge, mystery, forgiveness, the rise and fall of civilizations and people, poetry, stories of prophets, kings, disciples, war, disasters, the most fundamental and eternal truths, the end of the world, prophecies, songs, stories of bravery, how to live daily, and the best story of all—the story of our Savior.

What do you want to write? Search in the appropriate category and read all you find on that subject. The following are a few examples of some of those categories in the Bible.

HUMOR

Psalm 37:13 says, **"The Lord laughs at him, for He sees that his day is coming."** (NKJV) God laughs at men because of the futility of some people's efforts. Yet it is evident in the Bible that the Lord has humor.

Look at God's creation. Imagine the fun that the Lord had in creating some of His creatures. Have you ever watched an albatross fly and then land? That bird is graceful and beautiful when flying, but when it lands, it falls all over itself—every time. What about an opossum? Have you ever seen one play dead? I can tell you from experience that it is hilarious. When I lived in the mountains, every night I fed our cat outside on the porch, but soon after feeding, the cat would be still meowing for more food. One night I was determined to see what was happening, so I stood by the window, and what should appear? An opossum—and I watched him eat all the food. I ran outside before it could leave, but the second that opossum saw me, it turned on its back, feet in the air, with his tongue hanging out. I touched it with the broom, and it still did not move. What drama. What antics. God gave creatures some funny ways. What about the way a penguin walks? Think about an elephant with its long nose, a monkey with its humor, a parrot who mimics. Yes, I would say the Lord had a great sense of humor when he created animals.

Let's look at some humorous stories in the Bible.

1. Aaron and the Golden Calf

In Exodus 32, Moses had just returned from being with the Lord at Mount Sinai. He was gone for some time, and he had left Aaron in charge of the Israelites. Upon Moses' return, he saw that Aaron had made a golden calf for the people. Moses was angry. He confronted Aaron as to why he did it. Aaron's response was that the people were **"set on evil."** They wanted a god, so Aaron told the people:

"**Whoever has any gold, let them break it off.'** [Aaron looked at Moses and said:] **So they gave it to me, and I cast it into the fire, and this calf came out!**" (Exodus 32:24 NKJV)

How lame was that answer? I wonder if the Lord had a good laugh at Aaron's response.

2. Jesus and His Puns

Try as they might, the Pharisees could not get the upper hand over Jesus because of His wisdom and puns. One of my favorites is when Jesus called the Pharisees "blind guides." That pun says it all about them. The Lord uses the mastery of His Words throughout the New Testament.

The Lord has humor, and so should we. Many speakers begin by telling a joke because it breaks down walls so the people can listen. Humor does the same for writing. The Lord is never to be laughed at nor should His name be used in vain. Use humor in a good way. Thank God for humor.

ROMANCE

Another category in the Bible is romance. Many love stories can be found in the Bible: Isaac and Rebekah, Jacob and Rachel. My favorite is in the Book of Ruth—the fascinating love story about Ruth and Boaz. Ruth was bold, lovely, enterprising, and a determined young woman. The plot is wonderful.

Naomi's (Ruth's mother-in-law) husband, Elimelech, died, and then her two sons, Mahlon and Kilion, died. After Ruth's husband died, she would not leave her mother-in-law.

Ruth left her homeland and family to follow Naomi to a strange new land called Bethlehem. She was obedient to Naomi's guidance, even when it came to love. What a husband Naomi found for Ruth. Boaz was wealthy, respected, and intelligent, and he fell in love with

Ruth. He saw the kindness Ruth extended to her mother-in-law and how she labored in his fields daily. Boaz and Ruth submitted to God's plan, married, and had a son named Obed, who became the grandfather of David, who later became king, a man after the Lord's heart. Through his lineage, generations later, Jesus Christ was born. Now that is a love story.

The greatest love story in the Bible is the love relationship between the Lord and man—from when man fell and walked away from God, to the way that God showed man that this relationship could be restored through Jesus. The Bible gives us guidelines on how to grow closer to the Lord and each other—all out of His deep love for us.

CHARACTER IDEAS FROM THE BIBLE

Some picture must be given of characters for readers to visualize such things as their appearance, demeanor, mannerisms, and behavior. Study characters in the Bible. I actually patterned one of the characters in my book, *The Chosen Path*, after John the Baptist. He is the messenger named Kieran. By studying the way the Bible tells stories, writers can grow and become inspired to write their own stories. The following is a character sketch of John the Baptist.

John the Baptist

Name means: "Yahweh has been gracious."

Parents: Born to elderly parents, Elisabeth and Zacharias. John the Baptist was the second cousin to Jesus. He was filled with the Holy Spirit in Elisabeth's womb.

Home: He was born and raised in the town of Judah, but lived most of his life in the Judean desert, near the Jordan River. He was basically a hermit. In the Judean desert, there were six cities, which is where he preached. He was so anointed that the people came to him.

Clothing: His clothing was made of camel's hair and he wore a leather belt around his waist. John wore the prophetic dress of Elijah (see II Kings 1:8). So John had been designed under the name of this prophet, whose spirit and qualifications he possessed (see Luke 1:17).

Food: mostly locusts and wild honey. This might sound like strange food to us, but locusts were considered clean, simple food in the desert and are still eaten in that part of Judea today. John just ate the food that was available where he lived.

Occupation: Prophet and Preacher

Prophet: His ministry, like Jesus, did not come forth until he was about thirty years old. It had been three hundred thirty years since there had been a prophet (the last was Malachi). Malachi also prophesied that John the Baptist would come: **"See, I will send you the prophet Elijah before that great and dreadful day of the LORD comes" (Malachi 4:5 NIV).**

Preacher: John the Baptist was a priest of the order of Aaron, yet we find him preaching repentance and baptizing people in a wilderness, but he never officiated in the temple. His life's message was to prepare the way for the Lord. **"It is he who will go as a forerunner before Him in the spirit and power of Elijah, to turn the hearts of the fathers back to the children, and the disobedient to the attitude of the righteous, so as to make ready a people prepared for the Lord" (Luke 1:17).**

Personality: He was fearless—no man intimidated him. He spoke what he knew to be true, which eventually caused his death. He told King Herod he should not be married to his brother's wife and was later executed for it.

PLOT

Research the many plots in the Bible for help in formulating one for a book. For example, in the Book of Esther, Haman and his wife, Zeresh, instigate a plot to kill all the Jews, but Queen Esther foiled the plan. Genesis 37:18 speaks of the conspiracy of Joseph's brothers to slay him. Though Joseph was not slain, he was sold into slavery but was later redeemed and was put in a position to help save the nation of Egypt and his family. Another plot was when Judas made plans to kill Jesus. The plot worked, but only because God allowed it. What seemed like the biggest loss to mankind was the most triumphant of all. The Lord died so that we might live. Ideas abound for stories in the Bible, such as the following.

Catastrophes

Only eight people in the world survived the greatest catastrophe that ever happened on earth. Because of his obedience to the Lord, Noah and his family survived the most devastating flood ever. In another story, Sodom and Gomorrah, Lot, the only righteous man in the city, and his two daughters lived even when their city was destroyed.

Miracles

Miracle after miracle occurs throughout the Bible. Moses, Elijah, Elisha, and many others, performed astonishing miracles. Jesus healed the sick, the lame, and the destitute because of His compassion. He fed the hungry not only with physical food, but also spiritual. He loved children and blessed them. Through His treatment of others, a pattern was set for us to follow. He was the best Teacher of all—using examples people could relate to. The wisdom of His words ministered to the needy, captive, and lonely. He saw in people what others could not see and He forgave and redeemed many. He so loved the lost that He died for all and rose so that we might live with Him.

POETRY

Song of Solomon is a love story of the deepest kind, written from one lover to another. One can understand from reading it the depth of love that the bride has for her Bridegroom. The Psalms contain some of the most passionate poetry from the heart of man.

SEARCH THE BIBLE FOR TOPICS

While reading the Bible, watch for anything that draws your attention. Ask questions like these: What does it mean? Why is that important? Search, dig, and find; your passion will then be ignited for the subject. Keep a journal and write down anything you discover—Scriptures, revelations, anything new. Pray about what you have found, and ask the Lord for more. He may give you dreams—always be ready to write when you receive anything new. By keeping a record of what you are learning, you may find that more revelation will come. Soon you will have enough for an article, maybe even a book.

"Ask, and it will be given to you; seek, and you will find; knock, and it will be opened to you.

"For everyone who asks receives, and he who seeks finds, and to him who knocks it will be opened" (Matthew 7:7-8 NKJV).

GOD'S THOUGHTS

I want to know God's thoughts; all the rest are just details!
~Albert Einstein

God's thoughts launch us into writing. His inspiration—His breath—can flow through our words. We just need to be open to hear, receive, and write down what is given to us. We all want to leave a legacy behind. The written word will be here to be read over and over in the coming generations long past the time we are here. Make it the best it can be.

God is passionate in all He does. A tremendous opportunity stands before inspirational writers to put thoughts into words that truly inspire those reading them. But thoughts will only remain thoughts unless they are written. Dr. Norman Vincent Peale said this: "Action is a great restorer and builder of confidence. Inaction is not only the result, but the cause, of fear. Perhaps the action you take will be successful; perhaps different action or adjustments will have to follow. But any action is better than no action at all."

Do not let your inspiration dwindle to nothing. Keep your passion alive and write.

If you read history, you will find that the Christians who did most for the present world were precisely those who thought most of the next.

~ C.S. Lewis

Chapter Fifteen

Editors, Agents, and Manuscript Formatting

Manuscript: something submitted in haste and returned at leisure.

~Oliver Herford
Writer, artist, illustrator

When your manuscript is finally finished, it is time to submit it to a publisher. Unknown writers must be extremely careful with their first published work because readers and publishers alike will judge their work as good or bad in the very beginning of a writer's career. The first manuscript can make or break a writer. This may not seem fair, but it is true. If the book is published and does not sell well, the publisher will be hesitant to publish that writer's work again. Every effort must be made for the first manuscript to be outstanding.

As an editor, I see both unskilled and skilled writing. I see writing with outstanding themes, but the writer could not articulate the words powerfully enough to substantiate those themes. I see writing that goes round and round—the author wrote a page, when it would have been better written as a short paragraph. I have heard it said that some books should be articles and some articles should be books.

Knowing when to expound and when to end writing is a necessary skill. This comes through plenty of practice. Again, skilled writers have become wordsmiths, knowing how to use words in the most effective and powerful way. They have also mastered the basics of writing, applying those skills profoundly.

Many unknown writers submit manuscripts daily to publishers, hoping that their manuscripts will make it to the top of an editor's stack. If a writer is unknown, it will most likely go to the bottom of the pile. Typically, if an editor recognizes an author's name, his or her manuscript will go to the top of the pile. Why? It is an editor's job to know the published author's track record—the way he or she writes, how well their books sold, and the difficulty or ease of working with that writer.

However, every published author was a new writer once. If you are an aspiring writer, get to know people in the publishing field. Go to writer's conferences and meet publishers. Get your foot in the door so to speak. Another way to become known in the publishing field is to get articles published. An article is far easier to get published than a book, but it is still a helpful writing experience and looks good on a resumé. If unknown writers can ask well-known authors to endorse their manuscripts, these endorsements should be sent with the manuscript. A blog, which is basically an online journal, is another way for writers to become known. Beginning your own website aids in getting experience and exposure in writing. Some writers hire agents to promote their work. Bottom line: Do what it takes to get known in the publishing field.

AN EDITOR'S JOB

I have been a professional editor and published author for nearly ten years. What I am about to share is from my personal experience. Perhaps by understanding an editor's job, aspiring writers will have more patience in receiving an answer about submitted manuscripts for publication.

Publishing can be a slow industry. Be prepared to wait for months once your manuscript is sent to a publisher. Schedules for projects in a publishing company can span months or even years. An editor is already involved in projects with deadlines that are approved for publishing, and those usually take top priority over anything new. Editors do not have the time to stop and look at manuscripts that arrive daily. I spend more than 80 percent of my time editing. The rest of my time is spent in administrative work, meetings, and looking at potential manuscripts. Some time must be given to potential manuscripts for publishing, but most editors already have a steady flow of work from repeated and established writers. Again, those will take priority before unknown writers.

Manuscripts must meet certain criteria. The two main reasons for rejection of a manuscript are poor writing skills and old ideas. A sloppily written cover letter and poorly presented manuscript are deterrents as well. If a writer does not show care in presentation, there is a good possibility that the manuscript is just as poorly written. After you have taken the time to finally finish a manuscript, take the time to present it well. Formatting of manuscripts is covered later in this chapter.

WHAT EDITORS ARE LOOKING FOR

Editors read so many manuscripts that they can easily spot what makes a good book. Looking at the first page of the manuscript gives an editor a good idea about what the manuscript will be like. If the first page does not grab an editor's attention, usually there is no need to read further. Why? If a writer does not even know one of the most basic rules in writing, which is grabbing the reader's attention right away, then most likely many other basic writing skills are lacking.

Again, a manuscript must be in the best shape possible before it reaches a publishing company. Most aspiring writers become so excited that when they finally finish a book, they send it too fast to a publisher. Since you know it may take months for an editor to even look at a manuscript, take the time before submitting it to get it clean and concise. Remember this: Writing is the *most effective* with the *least amount* of words. Every time a manuscript is rejected, there is one less potential publisher of your manuscript.

Many articles and books are submitted that are worthy of publishing because of the fresh content, but if they need a great deal of editing, they will still be sent back to the writer. Editors just do not have time to work with someone who submits a poorly-written manuscript. Do everything possible to get your manuscript fresh, exciting, error-free, and polished. Again, an article or book that is well-written will take precedence over one that is not. Chances are if the manuscript is exceptional, eventually it will get published.

I have had writers tell me beforehand that nothing can be changed in their manuscript. I tell them as nicely as possible to look elsewhere to have their manuscripts published. All manuscripts will need some changes.

Through the years, I have learned to quickly look for what makes an article or book exceptional. Foremost, it is a well-written, fresh, and creative manuscript—something that will fit the needs of readers. It could be written in a distinctive or creative way, or perhaps the topic is unique, but most importantly, enthusiasm and passion ooze from the writer's pen. The pull to finish the book continues to the end.

An editor is looking for the following:

In non-fiction:
- Does it grab the reader's attention right away with a hook?
- Do the chapters build after the introduction in the book?

- Is it a page-turner?
- Is it well-written?
- Is it timely?
- Is it fresh with new insights?
- Does it have a strong and memorable ending or conclusion?

In fiction:

- Is there a hook with a dramatic scene in the beginning?
- Do the main characters come alive at the beginning?
- Is it a page-turner?
- Is the plot strong throughout?
- Is the problem solved? Are loose ends tied up?
- Is the conclusion memorable?

If it is an article, it should be a page-turner with a strong introduction, points well made, and memorable conclusion.

If an editor sees potential in a manuscript, he or she will work with the author discussing ideas about revision. An editor will look for improvements that will make the manuscript more effective. The writer needs to be open and listen to the editor's thoughts and possible changes. If a writer is too difficult to work with, chances are the manuscript will not be published. Most revisions suggested by the editor will need to be made, but if the writer does not agree with one or more, these can be respectfully discussed with the editor. Perhaps a compromise could be made. A good editor has the experience to see where problems occur in a manuscript and can help the writer improve it.

As an editor, I typically send manuscripts back with areas that need work and specific reasons why it could not be published as is, only to have some returned with little change. If an editor returns a manuscript with recommended changes, by all means work on every part, even if it means rewriting the whole manuscript. Be prepared to work on your manuscript again and again before publication. All editors have their own taste and skill in editing. A gifted editor is able to edit an author's work, while maintaining that author's style of writing. For an editor/author relationship to work there must be trust with both parties. Bottom line: If your writing has an intriguing theme, do not lose a chance at having it published by sloppy editing and proofreading.

TYPES OF EDITORS

Let's shed some light on an independent editor and an in-house professional editor's job at a publishing company. An independent editor works for and is paid by the author. An in-house professional editor works on the publisher's behalf, editing various authors' manuscripts that will be published by the company. Both typically have different areas of genre specialization from their experience. However, some editors possess the skills to work on all types of genres.

Editors can help writers with the following:

- Critiquing or manuscript evaluation, which is an assessment of the strengths and weaknesses. General suggestions are usually made.

- Content editing is another level offered. The editor looks for such things as style, structure, and specific problems like flow, unrealistic dialogue, and poorly-developed characters.

- Another aspect is line editing, which focuses on word use and sentence structure.

- Copy editing is when the editor corrects common errors in areas such as punctuation, grammar, and misused words.

- Proofreading is another aspect, which is when the proof-reader looks for typos, spelling errors, and so on.

An independent editor can either make suggestions or actually change them in the text, depending on what he or she is hired to do. The writer must decide what level of editing is to be done and will in turn pay for the editor's expertise according to the level of editing requested. Independent editors can be expensive, so be sure a business arrangement is signed to your satisfaction before any work begins. An independent editor is highly recommended when a manuscript is being self-published and will not have the advantage of a professional editor's skills in a publishing house. Before you hire an independent editor, make sure he or she is experienced. Request a resumé, references, and titles of works that the editor has edited. Check out the references.

Publishers have certain standards that must be met by an in-house professional editor. It may help to have an independent editor clean up a manuscript beforehand, but there is no guarantee if an independent editor is hired, that the publishing company will automatically approve it for publication. An editor can only do so much. The manuscript must have possibilities before an editor can polish it. Silver plate will never turn into sterling silver no matter how much polishing is done. An editor cannot guarantee publishing, even after the author and editor have worked on a project extensively. An editor cannot promise that a book will become a bestseller. That is up to the content of the book, readers, and how well the book is promoted.

AGENTS AND PUBLISHERS

If you want your book to be published by a large publishing house, hire an agent. Editors at large publishing companies receive thousands of manuscripts yearly. They simply do not have time to read every manuscript that is sent to them, and some do not accept unsolicited manuscripts. If a manuscript is submitted to them by a well-known literary agent, then the editor can have some assurance that it has been read by the agent who is promoting it and it should be considered. Also, if a literary agent is promoting a manuscript, then it should be in polished form.

All literary agents are not the same. They typically have a thorough understanding of the publishing market and know which publishers are best to promote certain genres. They also have good contacts and can promote a book in many venues. Some provide editorial help and some do not, so be sure to ask. Most literary agents have a genre that they prefer to promote. Research and find the one that best suits your manuscript. Even if a literary agent is not well-known, and if the author would like a manuscript submitted to a large publishing house, it still has a better chance of being considered than submitting an unsolicited manuscript. I know this may seem unfair, but you must remember—thousands of people are trying to get their manuscript published; editors have desks full of manuscripts. They want some guarantee before they read a manuscript that they are not wasting their time.

LETTER OF INQUIRY TO AGENT

The best way to approach an agent is through a letter of inquiry with a synopsis of your manuscript. Do not send the entire manuscript; send only the first three chapters. Send a self-addressed, stamped envelope for easy return with the agent's reply. If the agent is interested and wants to read your manuscript, he or she will contact you. When that happens, remember that the agent may have many clients, and to take on someone unknown is always a risk. Be open to suggestions from an agent with graciousness.

Most likely the agent will ask for a payment to read your manuscript, which should be discussed beforehand. If the agent offers a written criticism, it will likely cost more. It may take some time before a critique is given an offer of interest or non-interest in working on the project. He may ask some others to read it as well. Be patient. You have to remember that the agent is working with many authors. If the agent decides to help get your book published, he or she will help with the contract at the publishing house. As payment, most agents receive a flat sum or percentage from the sales after the book is published as payment.

How Do You Find an Agent?

Borrow library books or buy some books of well-known authors in the genre in which you are writing. Authors sometimes thank agents in their books on the acknowledgment page, which is another way to find an experienced agent. Talk to other writers—word-of-mouth is by far the best promotion of an agent. Do a search on Google for an agent, or agency and read everything you can about them. If they are reputable and have been successful with promoting books, then proceed forward with the process that you have just read above. Usually on their websites there will be submission guidelines.

To discover more about agents or agencies, attend writers' conferences and meet some publishers. As with any work field, you must get to know those who might help you to become successful. This will take time to build trust between both parties. Do not give up.

If you do not want to go with an agent, then something else needs to set your manuscript apart from the others submitted to a publishing house. The best way for publishers to read your work is for someone they know to recommend it. First-time writers are many, and if you are unknown, the chances of getting published dwindle. Build relationships in the publishing field. It sometimes is who you know that will help you get your foot in the door in the publishing world.

LETTER OF INQUIRY TO PUBLISHER

If you choose to ask a publisher rather than an agent to help get your manuscript published, certain steps should be followed. As mentioned, it is a time-consuming process to read manuscripts and articles, so editors do expect certain criteria to be met before the material is read.

Send a letter of inquiry to a publishing house *before* a manuscript is sent. Do some research and find out which publishers are publishing in your genre. When you discover those publishers, use their guidelines for submission. They will most likely want a letter of inquiry including a bio (editors are interested in knowing about the person they may be working with), experience in writing and publishing, endorsements, and a *brief* synopsis of your book (no more than one page). Show care with your letter, and be confident to make a good first impression. Above all, send an error-free letter.

If one or more publishing companies write and want to see more of your manuscript, send it to the one you like best. If that company is interested, continue with the process, but do not work with two publishers at once. Professionalism is a must in the publishing business. If more than one publisher is interested, let the one who you do not decide to use know that if it does not work out with the other publisher, you will contact them. If a publisher has shown interest in your writing, give them at least two months to respond. After three months, write a professional letter, asking the status. However, do not pester an editor. You will be contacted in time.

PREPARATION OF THE MANUSCRIPT TO SEND TO A PUBLISHER

The appearance of the manuscript clues the editor as to the professionalism of the author. If the manuscript looks neat, then that is one step in the right direction of a good impression.

1. If a publisher requests the completed manuscript, it needs to be easy to read. Use a simple, classic font like twelve-point Courier, where all letters are the same width. Times New Roman is also acceptable because it is also a classic font. Use one-inch margins with double-spacing, and do not justify the text, but indent each paragraph.

2. The manuscript should be printed on standard-weight white paper—not colored paper.

3. Use one space after punctuation, not two. This rule is implemented now by most businesses.

4. At the top left corner, type your name, address, email address, phone number, and word count for the manuscript. On all other pages, put your name and phone number. Cover letters can get lost, so make sure you do this.

5. Do not include a copyright symbol. It says to the editor that he or she might steal the story, which is an unsuccessful introduction to your manuscript. If you feel you must have your manuscript copyrighted, do it privately.

6. Insert page numbers on each page.

7. Attach a cover letter, single-spaced. In this letter should be a brief summary of the book's genre and story, with your contact information.

8. Include a one-page bio with published books, articles, and any unique qualifications.

9. Some publishers will accept emailed versions of manuscripts. Contact the publisher first before doing this.

10. Always make sure you keep a copy of your manuscript on file. Never send the original with no backup.

Publishing a book is a risk. Publishers need to make sure that they will get back the money that they invest in your book as well as make a profit. That is why a potential manuscript needs to be exceptional and in the best shape possible. Your first published work will set the bar for future published works. Take your time.

The effectiveness of literature depends upon the diverse skills of many different kinds of writers as well as the expertise of publishers, editors, artists, graphic designers, printers, distributors, bookstore managers, publicists, and of course, readers. When those in the publishing field work together as a team, much can be accomplished.

IF YOUR MANUSCRIPT IS REJECTED

Failure is simply the opportunity to begin again, this time more intelligently.

~Henry Ford
American industrialist

Most writers have had their manuscripts rejected *many* times before their work is published. Be encouraged if this has happened to you because you have been given even more time to make your manuscript better. Abraham Lincoln said, "My great concern is not whether you failed, but whether you are content with that failure." We all have failed in writing; those who will eventually succeed in the craft of writing will rise up and begin again until they succeed. The editor will most likely tell you why your manuscript was rejected so learn from the advice and criticisms given. If it was rejected for content, errors, ideas, or poor writing, work on the whole manuscript again, honing, cutting, refreshing, building, whatever it takes, but keep working on it until you are more than satisfied with the results.

A rejection slip can be positive if you look at it in the right light. Those who learn from the rejection experience and determine to grow in the areas that need improvement will eventually write that amazing manuscript and have it published.

If you received a rejection letter that looks generic, then the publisher probably did not look at the manuscript. Move on and keep trying other publishers. The hardest rejection letter to receive is the one when a publisher has been working with you, but in the end has decided not to publish it. Many reasons could have attributed to this decision, but most likely the final revisions in the manuscript from the author did not have the zest needed to publish the work.

Once I worked with a writer who had a potentially good manuscript, but I sent it back two times so he could correct some serious flaws. The only reason our department took the time with this manuscript from the beginning was we knew this person and felt the manuscript had potential. Both times I took the time to write how I thought this manuscript could be improved, and both times, there was some change, but not enough. It was eventually rejected. No more time could be spent helping this author. Again, if an editor takes the time to give you suggestions that you agree with, make them.

Take heart—if you have experienced your manuscript being rejected, you are in good company. Do not give up on your dream. Many famous writers have had their manuscripts rejected, and some, many times. The following are examples of authors who have had their work rejected.

J.R.R. TOLKIEN

John Ronald Reuel Tolkien, better known as J.R.R. Tolkien, knew what it was like to have a manuscript rejected. To his great satisfaction, however, *The Hobbit* was published by Unwin Publishers in 1936 without being rejected first. Unwin paid his ten-year-old son to read it for a shilling to see what he thought about it—he loved it, and Unwin decided to take a chance and published it. To his delight, it soon became a bestseller. In the late 1930s, Tolkien began writing the now famous book, *The Lord of the Rings*. He gave Unwin Publishing first chance at publishing it. Believe it or not, it was rejected by a staff editor while Unwin was away on business in France. Young Unwin, who convinced his father to publish *The Hobbit,* was now an adult and working in the family business of publishing. He discovered that the manuscript had been rejected and wrote to his father. After reading the manuscript, he asked for permission to publish *The Lord of the Rings.* His father agreed, and they published the trilogy with international success.

DR. SEUSS

Dr. Seuss was born as Theodor Seuss Geisel. The working title of his first book was *A Story That No One Can Beat,* and it was rejected many times by publishers. Why? They all said that there had never been a story like his. It was so unique that they could not see the value and creativity in it. One day he was walking the streets of New York, and he ran into Marshall McClintock, a friend from his college days at Dartmouth, who had just been promoted children's editor at Vanguard Press. They talked for a while, and McClintock asked Geisel what he had under his arm. He told him it was a manuscript that had been rejected twenty-seven times. McClintock asked Geisel if he could read it. He loved it, and Vanguard decided to publish it, and the rest is history. Geisel wanted a penname, so he took his middle name Seuss and added Dr. to it because his father always wanted him to be a doctor. His first book was retitled: *And to Think That I Saw It on Mulberry Street.* Had Geisel been a few minutes earlier or later, he would not have run into his friend. It was destiny.

Dreams of having your manuscript published can only die if you let them. Dr. Seuss went on to publish forty-seven books in eighteen languages. His many books are cherished by children around the world. Three of his most famous are *Green Eggs and Ham, The Cat in the Hat,* and, my personal favorite, *How the Grinch Stole Christmas.*

ANNE FRANK

Anne Frank wrote a heartfelt and profound diary during the two years she and her family were hiding in Holland from the Nazis until they were betrayed by an informant and sent by freight train to their final destination of Bergen-Belsen. She wrote of the hope she had in mankind in the camp—that in spite of everything she and her family had been through, she believed that mankind was still good at heart. Eight months later, at the age of fifteen, she died at that camp where nearly thirty thousand Jews eventually died. Though she is gone, her words live on.

The first rejection of her book was because the editor felt that Anne did not have a "special perception or feeling which would lift the book above the 'curiosity' level." Unbelievable! It was later rejected fifteen times before Doubleday published it in 1952. With more than thirty million copies in print, it became one of the best-selling books in history.

BEATRIX POTTER

Beatrix Potter had a great love for animals and nature with a rich imagination as a child, and she spent many hours watching and drawing her pets. Two favorites were her rabbits, Peter and Benjamin, which she drew in clothing. When she was an adult, she began her professional writing career by designing greeting cards with illustrations of rabbits and other animals. She then decided to write a children's book containing illustrations with animals in clothing. Her first book was titled, *The Tale of Peter Rabbit*. She sent it to six different publishers, and they all rejected it. Because she believed in her work, she decided to have it printed herself from the income she had saved from designing greeting cards. She had the innovative idea of printing a small book on sturdy paper so little hands could hold it and view pictures on every page. She had two-hundred-fifty black and white copies printed, and they sold so well that in three months she had the same amount printed. She then submitted it once more to Frederick Warne & Co., a publisher who had once rejected her book but was the most courteous of all the publishers she had sent it to originally. They decided they would publish it if she would illustrate color drawings. She did. *The Tale of Peter Rabbit* was a great success and has now sold more than forty million copies in thirty-five languages. Beatrix Potter wrote more than twenty books in her lifetime.

FIGHT!

Far better is it to dare mighty things, to win glorious triumphs, even though checkered by failure . . . than to rank with those poor spirits who neither enjoy much nor suffer much because they live in a gray twilight that knows not victory nor defeat.

~Theodore Roosevelt

To win a war, many battles need to be fought and won. To write is a battle in many ways. A true story happened many years ago that illustrates the importance of knowing when and how to fight.

In the Spanish-American War, the American soldiers were trying to capture San Juan Hill. They were not having much success because the enemy kept pushing them back. The use of black ammunition powder kept giving their position away to their enemies, and the troops began to panic because so many men were dying.

Teddy Roosevelt was their fearless commander. He rode up in the midst of the battle on a horse named "Texas." He encouraged his men to keep fighting. Because Roosevelt displayed his bravery by exposing himself to enemy fire, the troops began to cheer him.

"Don't cheer, men," Roosevelt called out to them. "Fight! Now's the time to fight!"

I have thought about this story many times. There is a time to cheer, a time to reflect, a time to reminisce, and a time to plan, but there is also a time to fight. Fight for your dreams and keep them alive—no matter what obstacles come your way.

Winston Churchill said, "A pessimist sees the difficulty in every opportunity; an optimist sees the opportunity in every difficulty." Your thoughts can lead you down a road of despair or hope. Stay positive with focus and determination. Do not delay writing another day. If you have a dream to write a book, see it fulfilled. Richard Bach said: "Here is a test to find whether your mission on earth is finished: If you're alive it isn't." Use your time wisely. As long as you are breathing, there is still time to fulfill your dream.

All we have to decide is what to do with the time that is given to us. Little by little, we travel far.

~J.R.R. Tolkien

QUESTIONS AND ANSWERS FROM SUCCESSFUL AUTHORS ABOUT WRITING

L earning from those who have walked out their dreams as authors will give inspiration to aspiring and even published writers. I asked the following questions to three successful writers; their bios and insightful answers follow.

Rick Joyner is the founder, executive director, and senior pastor of MorningStar Fellowship Church. Rick is a well-known author of more than forty books, including his international bestseller, *The Final Quest,* which is soon to become a major motion picture.

Stephen Strang is the founder of *Charisma* magazine, an award-winning journalist, entrepreneur, businessman, and author. He is founder and president of Strang Communications Company.

Robert Whitlow is the best-selling author of legal thrillers set in the South and winner of the prestigious Christy Award for Contemporary Fiction. His first book, *The List,* was made into a full-length motion picture.

1. **What are the top five things that make a book so outstanding that you would recommend it to others?**

Rick Joyner—1) subject matter, 2) depth of understanding or revelation imparted, 3) clarity of articulation, 4) brevity of articulation—getting to the point, and 5) continuity of thought with one building on the other and leading to a specific conclusion.

Stephen Strang—A book is outstanding when it is unique, has brilliant thoughts, and adds something to the wealth of knowledge. Examples that come to mind would be *Good to Great* or *The Seven Habits of Highly Effective People.* Another marketing book called *The Tipping Point* is an example. Each of these books have such brilliant ideas that people talked about them.

Excellent writing—In the same way a movie or music is not widely accepted if it's not top quality; the same is true with writing. Sadly, most books are mediocre and not brilliant.

A topic that I'm interested in—To me books are what the author is interested in rather than what the public wants. A book on trends is much more successful than a book on the inner thoughts of an author unless that author has earned the right and the following to share such thoughts.

Look and feel of a book—Some books look cheap and amateurish. Others look professional. Even beyond that there is a certain look that we talk about in the book business where a book looks like a "big book." I know that the book buyers and retailers find this is very important.

Endorsements from others—If people I really respect rave about a book, that influences me.

Robert Whitlow—I'm a novelist, so I will answer for fiction works: 1) believable yet unique characters, 2) intriguing plot, 3) story pacing that carries the reader along, 4) smooth style that is grammatically correct and doesn't jar the reader out of the imaginary world, and 5) ending that pays off emotionally.

2. **Who have been your greatest influences in writing and why?**

Rick Joyner—Tolstoy—because of his ability to articulate with depth, insight, and revelation that gave illumination and purpose to people and their lives.

Stephen Strang—My greatest influence in writing has been Jamie Buckingham. Thankfully, we were able to get him on tape the year before he died. In fact, this reminds me that I need to listen to those tapes again.

Robert Whitlow—We are influenced by what we read. I include at the top of that group Ernest Hemingway and John Steinbeck. As to the craft of writing fiction, I benefited greatly from a book titled, *Self-Editing for Fiction Writers,* by Brow and King.

3. **How do you get ideas for writing?**

Rick Joyner—I seek divine inspiration for matters that are timely.

Stephen Strang—I get ideas for writing based on trends I see around me and the things that the Lord is impressing in my spirit.

Robert Whitlow—The concepts for novels have come by either inspiration (an idea received directly from the Lord) or a sanctified imagination (an idea coming from within myself). It is best to write what you know. Thus, I set my stories in the South and write about lawyers encountering a supernatural God.

4. **How much time do you spend writing (daily, weekly, etc.)?**

Rick Joyner—at least two hours a day, six days a week.

Stephen Strang—My primary occupation is not that of a writer, so I probably just spend four or five hours a month literally writing when I'm not working on a book or manuscript. So this question is really not so applicable to me.

Robert Whitlow—I try to write a couple of hours a day, but if I miss a day, I don't worry about it. The danger is in letting a week or more pass without writing. My goal is to write about 1,000 words a day.

5. **How many times do you usually have to rewrite a book before it is ready to be published and why?**

Rick Joyner—When I began writing, it was between seven and ten times. Now I am down to about two or three.

Stephen Strang—Regarding rewriting a book, I heard someone say that good writing is "rewriting." I think a book probably needs to be completely rewritten at least once by the author and then a major edit by an editor, so that would be a total of two rewrites. However, this would vary based on the author or publishing house.

Robert Whitlow—I enjoy editing and revising my work. Including self-edits, each book goes through four or five edits.

6. What is the greatest hindrance to writing in your opinion?

Rick Joyner—distractions.

Stephen Strang—lack of creative ideas would be the greatest hindrance or just general mediocrity. It would be the same reason why there's a lack of real leadership or outstanding new music.

Robert Whitlow—bad grammar and choppy style can destroy a writer's ability to communicate.

7. Have you ever had writer's block, and how did you overcome it?

Rick Joyner—many times. You plow through it. I think this is mostly caused by a combination of "the paralysis of analysis" and going on feelings. I write even when I don't feel like it and almost always break through this quickly.

Stephen Strang—I have had writer's block. I overcame it through discipline and just pressing through. Sometimes it's just good to put your notes in a drawer and just sit and write whatever is on your mind, and then put that in a drawer and the next day come back to it. You'll find what you thought was writers block, really wasn't, and what you thought was mediocre really was better than you thought. And then you get busy rewriting it, it will be a springboard to write the kinds of things you need to write.

Robert Whitlow—I occasionally experience writer's block. When that happens, I may spend time editing what I've already written or begin with a simple scenario and allow my characters to jump-start an idea.

8. **What has helped you the most to become a better writer?**

Rick Joyner—diligence, perseverance, hard work, and reading.

Stephen Strang—The best thing that has helped me to be a better writer is to have excellent editors. Every outstanding writer needs an outstanding editor.

Robert Whitlow—I have been greatly helped by books about writing—basically ongoing self-education.

9. **What is your recommendation for getting a manuscript published?**

Rick Joyner—Pray and fast because you will need God's help if you are not an already published and popular writer. Then be sensitive to open doors so that you can take advantage of them, and to those that are not, so you do not waste your time on them.

Stephen Strang—My recommendation for getting a manuscript published is to have an outstanding idea and angle and twist to market it. As a book publisher, we are often more open to ideas before the manuscript is actually written because we like to shape the manuscript. Also, we go with people who have proven reputations and a following. We also go based on relationships so it's good to get to know publishers and editors personally. Sending a manuscript "over the transom" is a pretty sure way to not get it published. I doubt that 1 percent of the manuscripts sent this way are ever published.

Robert Whitlow—Write a grammatically correct book with good style that isn't amateurish; then research the type of publishers interested in your type of book.

10. What is the best advice you could give a writer?

Rick Joyner—read.

Stephen Strang—The best advice is to get to know publishers and editors personally.

Robert Whitlow—Keep writing until you finish the book; then don't resist the need to revise it. A book can always get better.

Don't live life in doubts and fears. Spend yourself on the work before you, well assured that the right performance of this hour's duties will be the best preparation for the hours and ages that will follow it.

~Ralph Waldo Emerson

BIBLIOGRAPHY

Austen, Jane, *Pride and Prejudice*, Barnes and Noble Classics: New York, 2003.

Berg, Elisabeth, *The Handmaid and the Carpenter*, Random House: New York, 2006.

Dorsett, Lyle W. and Mead, Marjorie Lamp, *C.S. Lewis, Letters to Children*, Touchstone: New York, 1985.

Joyner Johnson, Deborah, *Pathway to Purpose*, MorningStar Publications: Wilkesboro, 2005.

Joyner Johnson, Deborah, *The Chosen Path*, MorningStar Publications: Wilkesboro, 2003.

Lewis, C.S., *The Lion, the Witch, and the Wardrobe*, HarpersCollins Publishers: New York, 1950.

Martindale, Wayne and Root, Jerry, editors, *The Quotable Lewis*, Tyndale House Publishers: Wheaton, 1990.

Mitchell, Margaret, *Gone With the Wind*, Pocket Books: New York, 1936.

Morrell, David, *Lessons From a Lifetime of Writing*, Writers Digest Books: Cincinatti, 2001.

Oxford Pocket Dictionary of Current English, Oxford University Press: USA, 2007.

Sabin, William A., *The Gregg Reference Manual,* Glencoe, McGraw-Hill: New York, 2001.

Shrunk, William, and White, E.B., *The Elements of Style,* Fourth Edition, Longman: New York, 2000.

Tolkien, J.R.R., *The Hobbit,* Houghton Mifflin Company: Boston, 1937.

Tolkien, J.R.R., *The Fellowship of the Ring,* Ballantine Books: New York, 1994.

The Chicago Manual of Style online: http://www.chicagomanual ofstyle.org

Venolia, Jan, *Write Right,* Ten Speed Press: Berkley, 1979.

Zinsser, William K., *On Writing Well,* Seventh (30th Anniversary) Edition, Collins, New York, 2006 reprinted by permission of the author.

ACKNOWLEDGEMENTS

This book is dedicated to the many people who enabled this project to become reality.

To my dear friend, Joni Ames, thank you for your insight and encouraging me to write this book.

To Deb Williams, I will always be thankful for your loving support and proofreading skills.

To Dana Zondory, who did an amazing job on the layout, and Kevin Lepp, for your artistic touch on the cover, thank you.

To Sarah Roach, Cheryl Anderson, my daughter Meredith, and my son Matthew, I greatly appreciate your proofreading expertise.

To my daughter Abby, thank you for being so patient and understanding for the many months I spent writing this book.

To my brother Rick, thank you for everything you taught me about writing. I will always be grateful.

Last, for those who have only dreamed of writing a book, my hope is that after reading *Write to Ignite* you will be inspired to begin that book today. Now is the time to see your dream fulfilled.

~Deborah Joyner Johnson

Our truest life is when we are in dreams awake.
~Henry David Thoreau